FIELD MANUAL

ALSO BY JOCKO WILLINK

WAY of the WARRIOR KID
FROM WIMPY TO WARRIOR THE NAVY SEAL WAY

WAY of the WARRIOR KID 2
Marc's Mission

WAY of the WARRIOR KID III
WHERE THERE'S A WILL...

WAY of the WARRIOR KID
THE COLORING BOOK!

MIKEY AND THE DRAGONS

WAY OF THE
WARRIOR KID 4
FIELD MANUAL

BY JOCKO WILLINK   ILLUSTRATED BY JON BOZAK

PUBLISHING

Way of the Warrior Kid 4 Field Manual published under Jocko Publishing, a sectionalized division in association with Di Angelo Publications INC.

JOCKO PUBLISHING
In association with Di Angelo Publications
4265 San Felipe #1100
Houston, Texas, 77027

Way of the Warrior Kid 4 Field Manual Copyright 2020 Jocko Willink. Illustrated by Jon Bozak.
In digital and print distribution in the United States of America.

www.jockopublishing.com
www.diangelopublications.com
www.warriorkid.com

Library of congress cataloging-in-publications data
Way of the Warrior Kid 4 Field Manual.
Library of Congress Registration

Hardback

ISBN: 978-1-942549-66-6

Facilitated by: Di Angelo Publications
Designed and illustrated by: Jon Bozak

First Edition

10 9 8 7 6 5 4 3 2 1

1. Children's fiction

2. Children's Fiction —Narrative —United States of America with int. Distribution.

This book is dedicated to the

Fallen Warriors

of

SEAL Team Three, Task Unit Bruiser:

Marc, Mikey, Ryan, Chris, and Seth.

CONTENTS

INTRO: **I AM THE LEADER** PAGE 1

SECTION ONE: **THE CODE** PAGE 13

SECTION TWO: **DISCIPLINE** PAGE 62

SECTION THREE: **THE RIGHT THING** PAGE 77

SECTION FOUR: **BUST 'EM!** PAGE 94

SECTION FIVE: **LEARN!** PAGE 122

SECTION SIX: **ATTITUDE** PAGE 147

SECTION SEVEN: **AWESOME EXERCISES** PAGE 183

SECTION EIGHT: **AWESOME FOODS** PAGE 196

SECTION NINE: **YOU ARE THE LEADER** PAGE 208

I AM THE LEADER

UNBELIEVABLE! I almost made it through a whole year of school without needing any help from Uncle Jake. Everything went pretty smoothly in eighth grade. I studied hard and I did well in all my classes–even after we had to do online classes from home. In math class, I learned about algebra, geometry, and probability. In English class, I read speeches, fiction and non-fiction books, and I wrote essays and reports. In history, we learned about America: settling the colonies, the Revolutionary War, the structure of our government, and about the Civil War. I had fun in science too, where we studied the scientific method, earth science, and learned all about atomic theory–we even did some cool experiments in the lab! And of course, there was art class where I got to draw–which I'm pretty good at and I got even better. I took all my classes seriously and worked hard–and I got all A's!

I also kept working out and doing jiu-jitsu and running–it was great! I'm getting stronger, faster, and bigger. I'm actually four inches taller than I was at the end of seventh grade! I've been hanging out with Kenny, Nathan, Nora, and now Danny, too, and we've had a great time.

So, what went wrong? Why would I need Uncle Jake?

Well, over the weekend before the last day of school, I was out for a run in my neighborhood when I noticed a kid waving at me from his front lawn. He kind of looked familiar, so I took a break from my run and went over to him.

"Hi," he said. He seemed very shy but nice.

"Hi," I replied back with a smile.

He waited for a moment—like he wasn't sure what he was supposed to say—cleared his throat, and spoke. "My name is Curtis. Curtis Blythe."

"Nice to meet you Curtis Blythe," I replied.

"It... it... it's nice to meet you too."

"I think I've seen you around, haven't I?" I asked. I realized I had seen him around school, but since we didn't have any classes together, I had never talked to him before.

"Yes," he replied, "I've been going to school here for two years. I've seen you around too. I've always been in the same lunch period as you."

"That's cool," I said. "Well, it's good to finally meet you."

He smiled. I could tell there was something else he wanted to say to me, but his shyness seemed to be getting in the way.

"You looking forward to going into high school next year?" I asked, trying to keep the conversation going.

He waited. He got an even more uncomfortable look on his face and then mumbled, "I'm not sure."

"That's too bad. What's going on?" I asked.

"Because I'm going to a different high school. My mom's job makes her move around a lot, so now we have to move away," he replied with a dejected look on his face.

"Well, I'm sure it will be cool. You can meet some new people, see more of the country... look at it as an opportunity!" I suggested.

He tried to smile a little bit. He nodded gently. Then he said, "There's something else too."

"What's that?" I asked.

"Well when I first moved here, I noticed that a lot of the time, you and your friends wore Warrior Kid t-shirts. I had no idea what it was all about—but you all seemed... really confident and... well... cool! Sometimes I would hear you and your friends talking about it too—being Warrior Kids—working out, doing jiu-jitsu, and earning money from starting your own businesses. It seemed EPIC! And, well, I thought maybe I could be a Warrior Kid, too. I could learn to be more confident. I could do epic stuff with you all. But now I'm moving away and I'll never get to do any of that."

"When do you leave?" I asked. I figured if he was around for the summer, we would have plenty of time to get him on The Path.

"I leave the day school ends. The moving van already took most of our stuff away and once we finish with school, my parents are picking me up and we'll be gone."

"Hmmm... let me think about it. One thing that we do as Warrior Kids is try to solve problems. I'll talk to you tomorrow."

We shook hands and he walked away. Now, to be perfectly honest, I wasn't exactly sure what to do. In fact, I had NO IDEA! But I did have an Uncle Jake! While I was at school, Uncle Jake had arrived to stay at our house for the summer. As soon as I got home, I planned to ask him what to do.

When I walked through the front door, Uncle Jake was there. It was so great to see him! He only had one year left in college, so this was probably going to be the last summer he stayed with us.

"How is it going, Marc?" he asked.

"Great. And it's great to see you!" I told him.

"I've been driving all day—and it's great to see you! Want to work out?" Uncle Jake asked.

"Absolutely!" I told him. "Let me go change."

"I'll do the same," he said.

I went upstairs and changed, then came back down and met Uncle Jake in the garage. He was already doing pull-ups. I waited till he finished, then I jumped on the bar and did some as well.

"I got all your letters. I'm proud of how well you're doing in school, in jiu-jitsu and with your business—and with life. You are definitely on The Warrior Kid Path."

"I'm doing my best," I assured him, "but I know I can do better. I still have a hard time figuring some things out," I confessed, thinking about Curtis.

"Like what?" Uncle Jake asked.

"Well... listen to what happened today..." I started, then explained the whole story about Curtis, about how shy he seemed, how he would be moving away soon, and how he wanted to become a Warrior Kid, but couldn't because he's leaving.

Uncle Jake listened, then he did some pull-ups.

"When does he leave?" Uncle Jake asked.

"In a couple days," I replied, "Right after school ends for the summer."

Uncle Jake nodded, then he did another set of pull-ups while he thought about all that I had just told him. When he finished, he dropped off the bar, looked at me, and said two words: "Field Manual."

"Field manual?" I questioned him, extremely confused.

"Yes. A *Field Manual.* You know what a field manual is don't you?"

"I have no idea, Uncle Jake, but I've got a feeling I'm about to learn," I said with a smile.

"Yes, you are," Uncle Jake confirmed, smiling back at me. "Yes. Yes, you are. A field manual is what they call an instruction book in the military. It teaches you *everything* you need to know about... everything you need to know."

"So it's a text book? Like a math or science text book?"

"Yeah. Kind of. But field manuals teach in a very simple, step-by-step process, that anyone can follow. It makes learning easy."

"That's an awesome idea!" I cheered. "You will write a field manual on how to be a Warrior Kid for Curtis! Then he can follow it and actually become a Warrior Kid no matter where he lives! AWESOME!"

Here Marc, let ME do all the hard work for you...

Uncle Jake's head tilted. Then he shook it back and forth, telling me *no*.

"No?" I asked. "Is that not the idea?"

Uncle Jake smiled. "It's close to the idea. But there is one major difference. I'm not writing this field manual for Curtis. *You are.*"

"ME?!?!?!" I blurted, stunned. "I'm still trying to figure out how to be the best Warrior Kid I can be! I can't write a book about it! I'm not good enough!"

"Yes. Yes you can," Uncle Jake said with confidence, "And writing it will make you a better Warrior Kid. I have had to help write some field manuals for the military.

Sometimes I wasn't sure I was the best person for the job either. But writing about a subject always made me better."

"So that's what I have to do?" I asked.

"You don't *have* to do it Marc. You *should* do it. It will help you. But more importantly, it will help Curtis. So... will you do it?" Uncle Jake asked.

Once again, Uncle Jake was guiding me and I knew I needed to listen. Even though I didn't think I was qualified to write a book, I had to try.

"I will do it. I don't know if it will be great, but I will do my best."

"I know you will. And it will be great."

8

The next day I went and met Curtis outside of his house and told him my plan. I explained how I would write a field manual for him to follow and I would mail it to his new address as soon I finished it.

"AWESOME!" he exclaimed with a big smile.

"No problem!"

The next day, after we finished our last day of school, I walked back over to Curtis' house to say goodbye. We shook hands and then I watched as he and his family drove off in a car packed with boxes.

When I got home, Uncle Jake showed me some real field manuals. There were some about operations and leadership—even one on how to change the tire on a HMMWV! There were other field manuals about first aid, land navigation—even about survival in the mountains or in the jungle. They were awesome.

So, I started writing. I wrote every day—and every few days Uncle Jake would check over my writing and give me suggestions for making my field manual even better. After three weeks of work, it was ready: The Way of the Warrior Kid—Field Manual.

I hope Curtis likes it and that it helps him. I hope you like it and that it helps you too.

Here it is...

WAY OF THE WARRIOR KID
FIELD MANUAL

THE CODE

Before I got on The Warrior Kid path, I didn't have a clue about what a "code" was. Turns out I didn't have a clue about a LOT of things. I stunk at math and pretty much everything else at school! I slept in every day. I couldn't do a single pull-up in gym class. I ate junk food all the time... and I was AFRAID—afraid of water and afraid of standing up for myself—especially to the school bully, Kenny Williamson, who tormented me every chance he got!

I just wasn't good at many things and the main reason for that was because I didn't try! The reason I didn't try was simple: I didn't know *HOW* to try.

That all changed when my Uncle Jake taught me the Way of the Warrior Kid and I learned the value of having a personal code. I call it The Warrior Kid Code.

WHAT IS A CODE

A code is simply a list of important rules to live by. These aren't the same as laws enforced by the police or the government. These are guidelines to help keep you on the right path in life. They help push you, help you to improve yourself, and help you overcome your weaknesses.

Being on the Warrior Kid Path means doing the right things as you go through life. It means doing things you know will help you become smarter, stronger, healthier, and better. It's also about helping other people get on The Path, because the more people that are on The Path, the better the world will be. Sounds like a big deal, right?!

Well, IT IS! And it can also be a lot of fun!

DIFFERENT CODES

Throughout history there have been many awesome codes created by tons of different groups. Uncle Jake showed me a bunch of them back during the summer after my fifth grade.

- The Navy SEALS have their code.
- The Army Rangers and United States Marines have their codes of conduct.
- The Knights of the Middle Ages had a Code of Chivalry. Even the Vikings had their own code.
- Did you know that the Bible has a code? It's called the Ten Commandments.
- Even some schools have codes. They say things like "Take responsibility for learning," and "Treat others with respect."

These are all really great codes—and totally worth checking out! Each one is unique to the group that it belongs to. I came up with the Warrior Kid Code after that first summer with Uncle Jake. In case you didn't know, my Uncle Jake is a Navy SEAL—he is a real warrior and I think he is the best uncle EVER. He helped me learn what it means to be a warrior and taught me the things I needed to focus on if I wanted to become a Warrior Kid. One of those things was to have a code to live by. That's when I came up with the Warrior Kid Code.

You can follow my Warrior Kid Code and even change it to fit into your life. You can add to it or subtract from it. In fact, you can change it any way you like. But just remember: codes are meant to push you to become smarter, stronger, healthier, and better!

WARRIOR KID CODE

1. THE WARRIOR KID WAKES UP EARLY IN THE MORNING.

2. THE WARRIOR KID STUDIES TO LEARN AND GAIN KNOWLEDGE AND ASKS QUESTIONS IF THEY DON'T UNDERSTAND.

3. THE WARRIOR KID TRAINS HARD, EXERCISES, AND EATS RIGHT TO BE STRONG AND FAST AND HEALTHY.

4. THE WARRIOR KID TRAINS TO KNOW HOW TO FIGHT SO THEY CAN STAND UP TO BULLIES TO PROTECT THE WEAK.

5. THE WARRIOR KID TREATS PEOPLE WITH RESPECT, DOESN'T JUDGE THEM, AND HELPS OUT OTHER PEOPLE WHENEVER POSSIBLE.

6. THE WARRIOR KID KEEPS THINGS NEAT AND IS ALWAYS PREPARED AND READY FOR ACTION.

7. THE WARRIOR KID STAYS HUMBLE, CONTROLS THEIR EGO, AND STAYS CALM. WARRIOR KIDS DO NOT LOSE THEIR TEMPERS.

8. THE WARRIOR KID WORKS HARD, SAVES MONEY, IS FRUGAL AND DOESN'T WASTE THINGS, AND ALWAYS DOES THEIR BEST.

9. I AM THE WARRIOR KID.

I. THE WARRIOR KID WAKES UP EARLY IN THE MORNING

Warriors do NOT sleep in. They wake up early and get a jump on the day. By getting a jump on the day you're able to get things done like homework, exercise, reading, chores, and more before anyone else has even started their day. My Uncle Jake wakes up way before the sun even rises! He gets a TON of important things done before most people have even opened their eyes!

To be a Warrior Kid you need to be disciplined. Discipline means doing what you are supposed to do, EVEN WHEN YOU DON'T WANT TO DO IT. Let's face it—no one wants to get out of bed early every single day. It takes discipline. It also means you have to go to bed early so you get enough sleep. If you go to bed early you can wake up early and start your day off in the most disciplined way possible!

I know what you're thinking. "Why would I want to get out of bed early when my soft, warm pillow and blanket feel so great?!"

Sure, getting up early every morning can be difficult. But Warrior Kids aren't afraid of difficult things. If this was about doing the easy thing, then EVERYONE would be a warrior. Being a Warrior is EARNED, it's about working hard to do the right thing—even when it's super difficult—like getting up out of that warm bed early in the morning!

THE ALARM CLOCK

Do you have one? Then use it! The alarm clock is a great way to get yourself into a pattern of waking up early. Ask your parents when they think is a good time to wake up, then set your alarm for that time. If you don't have an alarm clock you can ask your parents to give you an early wake-up call every morning. Think of it as *The Parent Alarm.*

Once that alarm clock sounds or your parents give you the wake-up call, GET UP AND GET OUT OF BED! DO NOT HIT THE SNOOZE BUTTON! I know what you're thinking, "This is the WORST idea ever, Marc!" But it's not. Just throw the covers off, sit up, and get out of bed. It can seem SUPER HARD to do but it's actually very easy. You just have to force yourself. You can do it. You are a Warrior Kid, after all!

After a few days, maybe a week, maybe even a couple weeks, you might not even need the alarm. You will have programmed your body and mind to get up early and get a jump on the day! It's awesome and you CAN DO IT!!

Warriors do NOT use a snooze button!

SNOOZE

2. THE WARRIOR KID STUDIES TO LEARN AND GAIN KNOWLEDGE AND ASKS QUESTIONS IF THEY DON'T UNDERSTAND

Have you ever heard the phrase "Knowledge is power"? Well, it's true! The more stuff you know, the more powerful your brain becomes. The more powerful your brain becomes, the more you're able to do whatever you want in life!

Guys! My brain is getting HUGE from all the knowledge I've gained!

Um, Marc, I think you're having an allergic reaction...

When you learn something, that information gets stored in your brain. It could be the solution to a multiplication problem you learn in math class. It could be the story of a famous World War I Flying Ace that you learn about in social studies. It could be a new armlock technique you learn in jiu-jitsu class—it could be the term "knowledge is power" that you read about right here!

When I started jiu-jitsu for the first time, I STUNK AT IT because I had ZERO knowledge about jiu-jitsu! But I kept taking classes and listened to my Coach. I studied the moves other kids used. I asked the kids who were better than me to teach me the moves they used to beat me. Before I knew it, I was gaining all kinds of knowledge about jiu-jitsu!! The more I learned, the better I did.

That knowledge was POWER—it gave me the skills and confidence to stand up for myself. My brain was sharper and quicker from trying to outsmart and out-maneuver my opponents on the mat. Pretty awesome stuff, right?! The same goes for EVERYTHING. Learning math, spelling, science, grammar, art—anything! Knowledge is POWER!

LEARNING OUTSIDE OF CLASS

Classes in school are great for learning. To learn in a class, you can't sit back and expect the teacher to do all the work. You have to study. You have to ask questions. You have to put in the effort. If you do those things, you can learn a lot in class. But you don't only learn in classes. If you pay attention, you can learn from life every day. People you meet and things you experience can teach you a lot. Look how much I've learned from Uncle Jake! I've even learned from other kids, like Kenny Williamson, Nathan James, and Danny Rhinehart—and they were all my enemies at first!

I learned tons about improving MYSELF from them. I learned that bullying is terrible because of Kenny bullying me. I learned that I needed to control my temper and emotions after realizing how much Nathan's teasing bugged me! I learned that I needed to control my ego badly after getting annoyed at the fact that Danny seemed so much better than me at EVERYTHING!

I LEARNED. I gained knowledge and I was able to take action and that action helped me become smarter, stronger, healthier, and better!

It doesn't matter if you learn from school, from a book you read, from a parent, a friend, or even an enemy—the knowledge you gain makes you better and a more powerful Warrior Kid. Knowledge IS power, and your brain is your best WEAPON!

ALWAYS ASK QUESTIONS

Learning is not easy. It takes hard work. It takes discipline. And it takes questions!!

Uncle Jake taught me I should never be afraid to ask questions and you shouldn't be afraid either. Even the smartest and most successful people in the world ask questions. Actually, one reason they are so smart and successful is BECAUSE they ask questions!

Are you bad at certain classes like I was? At pull-ups? At sports? Maybe you try to follow what your teacher or coach is telling but you don't quite understand it. When that happens, that is EXACTLY when you should ask a question.

Don't feel dumb. Don't feel embarrassed.

You just don't understand what you are being taught yet. That's okay.

I bet there are a bunch of other kids in the class that also don't understand but are too afraid—or don't care enough—to raise their hand. But they aren't Warrior Kids. Warrior Kids aren't afraid to ask for help. Remember, teachers are here to teach us. They want us to learn. Raise your hand and when the teacher calls on you, simply explain that you don't understand.

See, Nathan? If you don't understand something or have a question in class, you just raise your hand.

I have a question, Marc. Did you forget to put deodorant on today?

3. THE WARRIOR KID TRAINS HARD, EXERCISES, AND EATS RIGHT TO BE STRONG AND FAST AND HEALTHY

Just like knowledge is power, physical fitness is power too! And it's also not easy. It takes a ton of hard work, discipline, and focus to become strong, fast, and healthy. That's why Warrior Kids train hard, exercise, and eat right—because all of those things are super important in order to be physically fit.

You might be asking, "Why do I need to focus on being strong, fast, and healthy? I'm a kid! I just want to run around, goof off, play some video games, and watch TV!"

I get it. If you'd rather goof off, then maybe you don't care about being a Warrior Kid. Maybe you don't care about getting on The Path...

But you wouldn't be reading this book if that was the case, now would you? Boom!

EXERCISE

One of the biggest reasons to exercise is to make your body strong! We know our brain is the most important weapon we have, and the brain is part of our body. To keep our brain healthy, we have to keep our body healthy. Just like we want our brain to be smart so we can get things done, we need to make our bodies just as strong so we can get things done. Just like training the brain with reading and studying, you have to train your body with exercise. The more you train, the more powerful your body will be.

Uncle Jake tells me exercising is something Warriors need to do their entire life and starting young is important. He says exercise will improve your strength, coordination, endurance, agility, flexibility, and self-confidence! And guess what? He's right because it definitely did for me!

I've come SO FAR from where I was in fifth grade, before I got on The Path!

FLASHBACK FROM:

WAY OF THE WARRIOR KID

FROM WIMPY TO WARRIOR THE NAVY SEAL WAY

This is ME (Marc).

I'm the hot dog-eating champ in my house!

This guy can beat me in a foot race.

And exercising is TONS OF FUN. Speaking of tons—there are TONS of ways to exercise which means TONS of ways to have TONS OF FUN!

Let's look at some:

- Sports: soccer, hockey and field hockey, football, basketball, baseball, golf, tennis, bowling, cross-country, track, skiing, snowboarding, skateboarding, surfing, swimming, wrestling, gymnastics and more...
- Combat sports: jiu-jitsu (my favorite!), wrestling, judo, boxing, muay thai, sambo, and many more.
- Calisthenics—this is what my Uncle Jake calls "P.T." which stands for Physical Training: pull-ups, push-ups, sit-ups, burpees, squat-lunges, mountain climbers, jump planks, rock wall climbing, and more...
- Aerobic: running, bicycling, jumping jacks, jump roping, and more...

You're probably already doing a bunch of these sports and exercises, which is awesome! But when it comes to the more difficult exercises or the completely new ones, you should make sure your parents know before you decide to try them—and make sure there's an adult teacher in charge when you do them. I've had Uncle Jake and Coach Adam guiding me on all the fitness stuff I've learned. Warrior Kids don't put themselves at risk—they learn the right way! Remember that!

EATING HEALTHY

I want to remind you of something: being a Warrior Kid isn't about doing the EASY thing. It's about doing what's RIGHT no matter how difficult that may be!

This is important to remember when it comes to this part of being a Warrior Kid: Warrior Kids don't eat junk food!

HA! I told you being a Warrior Kid wouldn't be easy!

To truly be a Warrior Kid, you need to eat healthy. That means potato chips, corn chips, cheese puffs, cookies, brownies, cakes, donuts, ice cream, candy, pizza, french fries, onion rings, soda, and milk shakes, and A LOT of other foods are not Warrior Kid foods.

There's a good reason: all those foods are garbage! Yes GARBAGE! The reason: they do nothing to help fuel your body. They are processed by machines and filled with chemicals or sugar—or both—and they are definitely NOT good for you. Those foods make you weak.

Warrior Kids need food that makes them strong. I call them STRONG FOODS. Strong foods fuel you so that you can perform at your best. Strong foods feed your body and muscles so that they can repair themselves after pushing yourself with exercise.

Remember back in the first Warrior Kid book? I used to eat TERRIBLY. My lunch was either a hot dog slathered in ketchup and relish or a ham and cheese sandwich drowning in mayo with a bag of salt and vinegar chips. And I'd wash it all down with a super sugary fruit juice or soda, followed by a bunch of fudge-filled, frosted cup-cakes!

Uncle Jake saw me eating all that junk and wondered how I was able to walk, let alone try to do a pull-up (I actually couldn't do any pull-ups back when I ate like that). He told me all that sugar and processed food drains your energy and makes you sick! And he was right. I used to get so tired after I ate that junk that I would need a nap and feel like my stomach was my enemy! And that's not a good feeling! Ha!

Uncle Jake showed me what he ate, which was clean, nutritious, REAL FOOD... not JUNK FOOD. His lunch was grilled chicken with milk to drink. They both have protein and healthy fats that rebuild your muscles after working out. He also ate a salad loaded with vegetables, which has minerals and vitamins that are important to keep the body and mind healthy.

I've never met someone as strong and healthy as my Uncle Jake! As a Navy SEAL, he had to do some crazy stuff—pushing his body and mind to the limit! By eating healthy, real food, he made sure he succeeded and he made sure he SURVIVED! Uncle Jake is a true warrior and he's proof that a healthy diet of STRONG FOOD is super important.

What warrior wouldn't want to be healthy and strong like Uncle Jake?

4. THE WARRIOR KID TRAINS TO KNOW HOW TO FIGHT SO THEY CAN STAND UP TO BULLIES AND PROTECT THE WEAK

When I look back at who I was before I got on The Path, it's pretty obvious that I was kind of a wimp! I was a big ZERO when it came to standing up for myself and I certainly couldn't protect the weak—because I WAS the weak! I let Kenny Williamson ruin my life with his bullying and insults.

But then Uncle Jake showed up that summer and I got on The Path. I learned what it meant to be a Warrior Kid. Slowly I got stronger. Slowly I got smarter and soon I learned how to stand up for myself.

It felt great to stand up to Kenny and not only show him that I was no longer afraid of him, but to KNOW and BELIEVE inside that I was no longer afraid of him. I had CONFIDENCE and he knew that he wasn't going to intimidate me or any of the other kids in school while I was around.

But if you think it's easy to turn from a wimp into a Warrior Kid... you're dreaming!

TRAINING

Warrior Kids train. We train our bodies and we train our minds so that both of them are strong, agile, and resilient. You're probably saying, "Yeah, Marc, I know, you just covered all that in Warrior Kid Code #2 and #3!"

I did! But I'm talking about training so we can fight and stand up to bullies and protect the weak. And for that we need to train at martial arts.

MARTIAL ARTS

Martial arts are made up of techniques that were developed by experts so people can defend themselves. There are a lot of different types of martial arts, just like there are a lot of different Warrior Codes. They come from cultures and countries from all over the world and from different periods in history. Each one uses different skills and techniques.

Some martial arts like Taekwondo and boxing focus on striking your opponent with kicks or punches or both. Some, like jiu-jitsu and wrestling, use grappling and throws. They all have some strong points, but my favorite is jiu-jitsu!

Every martial arts takes tons of practice to get better at and it can be intimidating when you first start. When Uncle Jake first brought me to Victory MMA for my first day of training in jiu-jitsu, I was scared—I thought I was a DEAD MAN! You might feel like that too when you first start.

But you know what? Everyone else in the gym got through their first day of training and lived to tell about it. AND they're still going and getting better! AND every person at your jiu-jitsu class is going to help you get better and push you to be better and be more confident! AND you're going to meet some really great people and make awesome friends!

CONFIDENCE

You'll find as you continue going to jiu-jitsu that you're getting better. You'll be facing off with other kids to see if you can get them to tap out, while defending their attempts to get you to tap out. All of these skills are things you'll use in the real world to defend yourself—pretty awesome!

It's pretty simple: the more you practice the better you'll get. The better you get the more confident you'll become. Being more confident means you won't question your ability to stand up to a bully and defend yourself in a fight.

REAL FIGHTS

Fighting. Who would have guessed a book written by a kid that does "the right thing" would talk about fighting? Well, this is a book written by a Warrior Kid and it does. BUT—and this is SUPER IMPORTANT—Uncle Jake, a Navy SEAL who's fought in crazy battles and in wars against terrible enemies, taught me that fighting should absolutely be avoided if it is at all possible. If anyone understands the rights and wrongs of fighting, it's Uncle Jake! Fighting is very dangerous. People get hurt. Warrior Kids never fight unless they have no other choice at all. This might seem crazy, but the more prepared a person is to fight, the better they are at avoiding fights.

AVOIDING FIGHTS

It was easy back in sixth grade to think that fighting Nathan James was the best solution to stopping his nonstop insults.

If you read the second Warrior Kid book, you'd know that fighting was NOT the right way to deal with Nathan! So did Uncle Jake! He pointed out that I knew nothing about Nathan and even less about why he teased me all the time. Maybe, if I found out why, I'd come up with a better way to make him stop.

The first step was to detach from my emotions so I could think, see, and act clearly. The second was to start acting like a leader instead of like a baby. Once I did, I began to see more clearly why Nathan was trying to annoy me.

I found out that Nathan was super poor, only had dirty and worn out clothes to wear, and lived alone with his mom who worked hard for very little money and didn't have much time to spend with Nathan. In fact, he spent most of his time on his own. Nathan had a hard life and insulting people was the only way he knew how to talk to people.

Once I realized how bad things were for Nathan, and how lucky I was to have such a good life, I decided to help him instead of fight him. From that moment on, when he would tease and insult me, I didn't get mad. I laughed! I even poked fun at myself—which made us both laugh!

I have to admit, it was pretty funny when you used to joke about me having a weird-looking face.

Wait, you thought I was joking?

I showed him I was in control, not him. I was acting like a leader and Nathan needed a leader in his life. First, I helped him get a job at Victory MMA so he could earn some money and keep busy. Then I got him into jiu-jitsu classes. And soon... we became friends!

I followed Uncle Jake's advice and learned there were much better solutions than fighting. Just because I had learned how to physically defend myself didn't mean I needed to fight every time I came across a difficult person. I solved the difficulties with Nathan and I gained a pretty awesome friend!

DEFENDING THE WEAK

There are people that can't defend themselves. It's not their fault. They could be too young to even understand what defending themselves means or they could be too old and not have the strength to defend themselves. They could be sick or injured. They could simply just not know how to stand up for themselves.

I always remember how weak I was before I became a Warrior Kid. It stunk to be weak and powerless against bullies like Kenny Williamson!

Because Warrior Kids know how helpless it feels to be bullied, we have a duty to defend those that are weak. Warrior Kids don't just do things for themselves. As leaders we take care of the people around us, especially those that need our leadership and strength the most.

5. THE WARRIOR KID TREATS PEOPLE WITH RESPECT, DOESN'T JUDGE THEM, AND HELPS OUT OTHER PEOPLE WHENEVER POSSIBLE

Respect means you think about the way other people feel and try to treat them in a way that doesn't hurt their feelings. Imagine if someone you know—a neighbor, a classmate, a family member, or even a teacher—spoke to you like they thought you were stupid and always acted like every one of your ideas was dumb.

That's what it is like when someone doesn't respect you. It hurts your feelings.

What if someone else decided that you couldn't hang out with them at lunch or after school because they didn't think you were *cool* enough, or your clothes weren't *nice* enough, or your family wasn't *rich* enough...

How would that make you feel? Like they were judging you, right?!

All of this would probably make you feel sad. And mad. You might even feel like you weren't good enough. I can tell you those feelings are some of the WORST FEELINGS!

Remember how bad I felt when Kenny used to bully me around? When kids would make fun of me for not being able to do a single pull-up? Even if I WAS a wimp, it was still no reason for people to be mean about it.

Nobody wants to feel judged or like other people don't respect them, which is why Warrior Kids should never treat other people this way. It's super important to treat people with respect and to not judge them.

TREATING PEOPLE WITH RESPECT

Treating someone with respect means treating them fairly, treating them like equals, and treating them like they are important and that you value them. It doesn't matter if they come from a different school, a different state, or a different country. It doesn't matter if they are a different race, if they are a boy or a girl, if they are younger or older—none of that matters. Everyone deserves to be treated with respect.

35

Sometimes... we can mess up. When this happens, we need to apologize.

Remember when Danny Rhinehart first used the omoplata on me during jiu-jitsu? I knew he was about to submit me with it, but rather than be fair and allow him to win... I yelled out and faked that he had injured my shoulder so I wouldn't lose. He instantly let go, worried I had been hurt.

I carried on with the lie. I wasn't showing him the respect he deserved. He was better than me at jiu-jitsu and was about to earn a victory over me—but rather than being fair, I lied and denied him what he had earned fair and square.

It took me a while, and it took some conversations with Uncle Jake and Coach Adam for me to realize that I needed to apologize. Danny accepted my apology and it was one of the first steps to becoming super close friends!

JUDGING

I know I just said that Warrior Kids aren't supposed to judge people. But guess what? I'm guilty of it! It can be super difficult to not judge people if you get lazy with your thinking. Warrior Kids remember that nobody should judge another person. We can NEVER know the full story behind how and why they act or look or behave the way they do.

Look at how I judged Nathan as being sloppy because his clothes were a mess. I judged that he must be lazy and messy! But I didn't know the full story. I didn't know his mom didn't have enough money to buy him new clothes. She actually didn't have enough money to feed him properly! Nathan had it so bad! Once I found out the truth, I realized how WRONG my judging him was!

I also judged Danny as being too cool to ever come over and hang out with me after school. I had NO IDEA the reason he couldn't come over was because he had to go home and take care of his special-needs brother.

We can NEVER know the full story about anyone, which means we shouldn't make decisions or judgments about them.

HELPING OUT OTHERS

Warrior Kids are SUPER LUCKY! Why? Because we are on The Path. This means we are leaders. We are strong and we are smart and we care about doing the right thing.

This means helping other people out if we can. It's super simple. If you spot someone that needs help with something, you should do your best to help.

6. THE WARRIOR KID KEEPS THINGS NEAT AND IS ALWAYS PREPARED AND READY FOR ACTION

A LOT of kids think cleaning up after themselves and keeping their stuff neat and in order is a waste of time. They tell me things like, "Why should I bother cleaning up when I'm just going to make everything a mess anyway?" or "What kind of *warrior* worries about being *neat*?" and "It's a million times more fun to make a mess than to clean one up!"

Who can argue with all those points?!

Well, a Warrior Kid can!

Once I got on The Path and learned more about what it means to be a Warrior Kid, I started to understand how important it is to keep yourself organized and to stay ready for action. Let me explain...

KEEP IT NEAT AND ORGANIZED

Cleaning up after yourself is never THAT fun. And it usually comes AFTER you've done something fun, which means cleaning up reminds you that the fun is over—so it's natural to think cleaning up STINKS! It's a bummer!

Until you become a Warrior Kid...

Once I got on The Path, I learned that staying neat and organized isn't just about cleaning up AFTER you've made a mess. It's about keeping all the things in your life neat and organized ALL THE TIME. This will help you to do the things that you want to do—the fun things and the important things—much more easily.

So, our parents are always making us clean our room, right? And usually they're asking us to clean it because it's a total mess—and cleaning up a room that's a total mess takes forever! You could spend half a day or more cleaning a room that is super messy!

Imagine your room is a total mess and you need to find something important. Good luck! Whatever you're searching for is lost in the mess and it'll take forever to find it. But what if your room wasn't a total mess? What if you spent just a little time every day making sure it was neat rather than letting the mess build up. I'm talking maybe ten or fifteen minutes a day.

Well, then you'd only be spending ten or fifteen minutes a day to keep your room clean! No more half-a-day cleaning missions! And no more endless searches for stuff you need to find. That means you have a ton more time to do awesome stuff!

And it's the same for pretty much everything in life. Your school locker, your backpack, your backyard... everything!

BE READY FOR ACTION

I know you're asking me in your head, "Marc, exactly what kind of action am I supposed to be ready for?" Well, it's a good question and I have the answer: *EVERYTHING.*

As a Warrior Kid we need to always be ready for action in every imaginable situation, which means we can react confidently, quickly, and correctly in the moment—no matter what is happening.

Here's some examples of why it's important to be ready for action:

- What if there is an emergency and you need to leave your house? If you are organized, you can be ready super fast.
- What if someone gets a cut or a scrape and you need a Band-Aid really quickly? If you are organized, you will know right where they are.
- What if your friend needs to borrow your baseball glove for a game? If you are organized, you will know exactly where it is.
- What if you get a flat tire on your bike? If you keep things neat, you will know just where to find the pump.
- What if you get asked about a book you read, but you can't remember the answer? If you keep things neat, you will know precisely where that book is.
- What if there is a fire and you need to get out of your room quickly? If your room is clean, you won't trip over things trying to get out.

I could go on forever because these kinds of "*What if?*" questions never stop. That is why we, as Warrior Kids, need to stay organized and ready for action. If we fall off The Path, we stop being ready.

7. THE WARRIOR KID STAYS HUMBLE, CONTROLS THEIR EGO, AND STAYS CALM. WARRIOR KIDS DO NOT LOSE THEIR TEMPERS

Imagine you're hanging out with someone who's super-competitive over EVERYTHING and they refuse to ever admit when they're wrong. If anyone disagrees with them, they start sulking like a baby. AND if they don't get their way, they get so mad that they start screaming at the top of their lungs.

This sounds like the WORST person to hang out with, right?!

I agree! But guess what: the person I just described was me! Yes, me!

DON'T throw a temper tantrum like I did in sixth grade!

FLASHBACK FROM:
WAY OF THE WARRIOR KID II
MARC'S MISSION

That's exactly how I acted toward Nathan James when he was super annoying and kept saying super-annoying things to me at school during sixth grade. I mean… come on, I was so mad I wanted to fight him!! What a dummy I was!

But really, the reason that Nathan James got under my skin was because I LET HIM. I could have reacted very differently. I could have behaved very differently. But I just worked myself up, getting madder and madder at Nathan–even when he wasn't around!

Nathan James had control over my emotions! How crazy is that?!

Well, the good news is I learned that I have control over my emotions! And that means YOU can have control over yours! Maybe it's a brother or a sister that's trying to push your buttons. Maybe it's your parents telling you to do something you don't want to do. Whatever it is, you don't ever want to act like a baby and lose your temper.

Uncle Jake helped me to understand we all have the power to control how we react to things–and when we lose control over how we react, we make the situation worse.

It's not easy, but true warriors control their emotions, don't lose their tempers, keep their ego under control, and practice humility.

STAY HUMBLE AND CONTROL YOUR EGO

It's super important to always remember that Warrior Kids try to stay humble. Being humble or having humility means that you NEVER act like you're more important or better than another person. It means you don't let your ego get out of control.

Here's an example:

Imagine you're playing baseball and you're up to bat with the game on the line. You need to score for your team to win. The other team's pitcher is on the mound, and he's throwing some tough stuff! You dig in... the pitcher delivers their best pitch, you swing and... HOME RUN!!

A person who is NOT humble—who is NOT showing humility—would jump up and down and cheer as they round the bases. They might shout things like, "I'm number one!" and tell the other team's pitcher, "I got you!" They would try to draw TONS of attention to themselves and what they just did. That's bad sportsmanship. And that is A LOT of ego!

A Warrior Kid—like you and me—would do it differently.

I'm a HOME RUN HITTING LEGEND!!! Everyone else stinks!!

DON'T be that kid. Be humble. Be respectful.

A Warrior Kid would control their emotions after the home run and quietly round the bases. Maybe on the inside, they're totally freaking out! Maybe they're so proud of what they just did, they want to celebrate with everything they've got.

But they wouldn't.

That would be insulting the other players by drawing attention to their loss and failure. A Warrior Kid puts themselves in the other person's shoes and acts respectful.

Imagine if the tables were turned and YOU just pitched that home run ball… chances are you'd feel TERRIBLE! You wouldn't want the other players to start bragging and rubbing it in. When you understand how it feels to be THE OTHER GUY, you will understand how important it is to be humble.

This doesn't mean you can't be happy and celebrate. There is nothing wrong with those things. But Warrior Kids celebrate in a humble and respectful way because that is the way real champions act. It could be winning a baseball game, tapping out a jiu-jitsu opponent, acing a math test, baking a delicious cake, or just about anything. When you win, be proud! But remember that staying humble in the moment is the Warrior Kid way!

KEEP CALM AND DO *NOT* LOSE YOUR TEMPER

Imagine for a moment…

- Someone makes fun of you in front of all your friends and EVERYONE starts laughing at you.
- Your brother or sister gets angry at you for NO REASON and starts yelling at you.

- Your parents tell you to eat all the soggy vegetables on your dinner plate or they won't let you watch TV.
- Your brother or sister has an awesome snack and won't share it with you.
- Your parents just told you to clean your room or to brush your teeth or to go to bed—because they said so!
- You get grounded when you didn't do ANYTHING wrong!!

Each one of those scenarios sounds super annoying, right?! Would any of those situations make you upset? Mad? Maybe even make you want to throw a tantrum? You're probably nodding your head "Yes!" right now, aren't you?

I totally get it! It's hard to stay calm and control your temper when those kinds of things happen. But guess what: it's really important as a Warrior Kid to stay calm and control your temper no matter how annoying the situation!

Do you want to know why? Well, for one: losing your cool only makes the situation worse. That's right!

Getting mad, yelling, screaming, or stomping off only makes you look like a big baby. And that means everyone is going to treat you like a big baby—because you're actually acting like a big baby!

Losing your temper wastes your energy and your focus and stops you from seeing the situation clearly. All you can think about is how ANGRY YOU ARE! All you see is how mad that other person or thing is making you. But actually, YOU are making YOU mad. By focusing on being mad you aren't seeing the bigger picture.

DON'T be that kid—also known as ME—in sixth grade!

FLASHBACK FROM:

WAY OF THE **WARRIOR KID II**
MARC'S MISSION

The bigger picture could look like this:

- Maybe when you got made fun of and your friends were laughing—it was actually funny! Maybe the person who teased you was just trying to make you laugh!
- If your brother or sister gets mad at you for no reason, that's their problem! Just because they can't control their temper doesn't mean you shouldn't control yours.
- Maybe your parents are telling you to eat your vegetables because they're actually GOOD FOR YOU—and they want you to be healthy and grow up strong.
- If someone won't share an awesome snack with you... that's THEIR decision. You can't make people do what YOU want. But you can go find your OWN awesome

snack and maybe offer to share it with them so next time they WILL share theirs with you.

- Cleaning your room, brushing your teeth, and going to bed early are REALLY IM-PORTANT! Warrior Kids keep things neat, take care of their body, and take steps to wake up early.

- It stinks, but getting grounded means you did something wrong. Punishment is the WORST at first but think about what you are getting grounded for. Think about how your actions affect others and how to avoid doing it again. Your parents are trying to teach you right and wrong, and knowing what's right is super important to getting on The Path.

RED FLARES

You're probably thinking, "Okay, Marc, I get that I shouldn't lose my temper. But how do I stop it from happening? It's not that easy!!"

You're right, it isn't. You have to recognize when you're starting to lose your calm and change your reaction. And there's a great way to do just that!

Do you remember when Uncle Jake told me about "red flares" after my tantrums over Nathan James? Red flares are signals from your body that you can feel when you're beginning to lose your temper.

Signals like:

- Clenching your fist.

- Feeling your face turn red.
- The back of your neck getting hot.
- Your stomach getting tight.

Uncle Jake taught me ways to detach when I feel those red flares coming on, and they'll work for you too!

- Breathe. Tilt your head back and take 5-10 deep, slow breaths until you feel calm.
- Focus. Focus your mind on something totally different—things that make you feel good. Maybe a food you love, or a funny joke a friend told you, or imagine something that makes you feel happy, like petting your family pet, or sinking a buzzer-beater shot at basketball!
- Walk away. There's nothing wrong with walking away from a situation that causes you to lose your temper. Just remember, you might have to explain why you walked away later. This will give you a chance to calmly think about and discuss whatever it was that made you upset. That's actually a great thing!

8. THE WARRIOR KID WORKS HARD, SAVES MONEY, IS FRUGAL AND DOESN'T WASTE THINGS, AND ALWAYS DOES HIS BEST

Kids who don't know about The Path don't always get why it's so important to us Warrior Kids to work hard. A lot of kids think hard work is only for their parents and other adults with jobs and that kids shouldn't have to work. Some kids think that they should only have fun and goof off!

WRONG!

Uncle Jake told me that adults don't just suddenly figure out how to work hard when they become adults. They learned how when they were kids. School and classes can be hard work. Chores around the house can be hard work. Playing a sport or a musical instrument or learning a hobby takes hard work. Even not arguing with your brother or sister can be hard work!

Each summer that Uncle Jake visits, I learn more and more about why it's so important to work hard no matter what age you are and no matter what you're doing. AND that working hard isn't only about having a job that pays you money.

Here are some examples where I learned about hard work:

- Fifth grade: I learned the value of getting up early, doing push-ups, studying with flash cards, learning jiu-jitsu, and being disciplined.
- Sixth grade: I learned how to control my temper, how to fix up my bike, how to earn money and save it, and how to compete at martial arts competitions.
- Seventh grade: I learned how to control my ego, how to captain my jiu-jitsu team, and how to push myself beyond my comfort zone.

Learning how to do all those things was not easy! I had to apply myself. I had to focus. I had to do things that made me UNCOMFORTABLE. I had to be patient and believe that my efforts and discipline and HARD WORK would help me accomplish what I wanted.

What did I want? I wanted to be smarter, stronger, healthier, and better!

Who's psyched to be smarter, stronger, healthier, and better?...

THIS KID!!

Think about one goal you want to accomplish. Unless you want to be the chocolate-chip-cookie-eating champion of the galaxy, I bet accomplishing it is going to take lots of hard work! But if you put in the effort, push yourself, and stay disciplined you can reach your goal. You're a Warrior Kid and when Warrior Kids do something, they always try their best!

But, Marc it takes a lot of hard work to NOT eat these chocolate chip cookies too quickly!

Honestly, I'm not sure what to do with you guys...

TRYING YOUR BEST

You can work hard by putting in lots of effort, lots of repetition, and plenty of discipline. But you also have to try YOUR BEST.

I learned this the hard way during the summer after seventh grade when Uncle Jake and I worked on my running. In case you don't remember, I wasn't a huge fan of running… and I even told Uncle Jake that!

That didn't exactly go over very well! Nothing like trying to avoid doing an exercise you don't want to do with a Navy SEAL uncle!

Anyway, my goal that summer was to run a mile in less than six minutes. At the start of the summer, I couldn't even get under the seven-minute mark. With Uncle Jake's help, I discovered that I simply didn't know how to push myself. I wasn't trying my best when I ran. I worked hard. But I was staying in my comfort zone—trying hard, but not hard *enough*.

Guess what? That's not going to cut it when you're trying to shave a whole minute off your time!

I didn't understand how to try my best. Uncle Jake coached me how to push through the mental blocks and physical discomfort. Soon I was able to run a mile in less than seven minutes.

Once I realized how to push myself and try my best, I began to get better each time I ran. This is what's so awesome about trying your best—if you always try your best you are almost ALWAYS going to get better at what you're doing. How do I know? Because before summer's end, I ended up running a mile in less than six minutes. It was so awesome!

The same goes for trying your best at sports, school, hobbies—everything! Doing your absolute best becomes a habit. And if you try your best, you will get better. You will improve. It might take longer to get better at some things and not so long at other things, but in the end, you will be super proud that you never settled for your comfort zone!

BEING FRUGAL, NOT WASTING THINGS, AND SAVING YOUR MONEY

I bet you're wondering why The Warrior Kid Code even bothers to mention "saving your money." We're kids after all, right? It's not like we're rolling in cash! It's not like we're looking to head down to the local car dealership and leave with a new truck! Plus, our parents take care of all that money stuff, right?

Well, they kind of do. For now.

But... us kids are going to grow up and become adults and then we will have to take care of all that money stuff on our own.

Luckily, Warrior Kids start taking care of all that money stuff early...

FLASHBACK FROM:
WAY OF THE **WARRIOR KID III**
WHERE THERE'S A WILL...

Money can be a powerful ally!

I learned a bunch of lessons about money during the summer after sixth grade. I also learned to value and take care of the things I already owned.

It all started with me wanting the brand-new Bentlee bike, REALLY BAD! It was big, shiny, and just screamed "Best bike ever made in the history of bikes!" But it was PRICEY, and I didn't have any money to buy it. I figured I needed to find a way to get my mom to buy it!

Uncle Jake was not very impressed with my plan.

Maybe it was because I already had a bicycle my parents bought me in the garage.

Maybe it was because I had let that bike get all rusty and dirty and banged-up.

Maybe it was because my mom didn't have the money to buy me the Bentlee.

Actually, it was for ALL those reasons and more!

Looking back now, just like Uncle Jake wasn't impressed with my plan, I'm not impressed with my plan to get the Bentlee either! Not after I learned so many valuable insights that summer thanks to Uncle Jake. Here are some things I learned:

- Honestly, I only wanted the Bentlee because it was shiny and NEW and would make me look cool.
- I was taking my parents' generosity for granted. I expected that because they had jobs and money that they should get me whatever I wanted.
- Getting things for free doesn't teach you to appreciate their value—or the value of the hard work it takes to earn the money to buy them.

- I never valued the old bike I already had because I didn't do ANYTHING to earn it. I didn't spend a dime on it! Because I didn't have to work for it, I didn't care for it properly, and it ended up rusted with flat tires in my parents' garage.
- When you VALUE the things you have, you actually WANT to take care of them. And you don't crave new, shiny things just "because."
- By fixing up and customizing my old bicycle, which I named The Bruiser, it instantly became cooler than the Bentlee because all the hard work and effort I put into it made it MINE and more unique and way cooler than any store-bought bike.

FINANCIAL FREEDOM

The other awesome thing I learned that summer was how to earn my own money. That's the summer I started my own business, "Marc's Meticulous Mowing". Pretty crazy, right? Well, it's not that crazy! With every dollar I made, I was creating freedom for myself. I was no longer limited to relying on my parents for money. I was setting myself up to buy whatever I wanted–like the Bentlee! That is called financial freedom.

But I soon learned something important about the Bentlee. While I have to admit that I wanted it, I knew deep inside that I didn't *need* it... especially not once I had rebuilt and customized my old bike, The Bruiser!

By not spending my hard-earned money on things I didn't need–and following Uncle Jake's advice to ALWAYS SAVE 20% of every dollar I made–I was creating even MORE financial freedom! Now I had money saved for an emergency or a really important situation–which actually came up during that summer.

Do you remember what that situation was? It was helping Nathan James pay for jiu-jitsu lessons because he and his family had no extra money for it. This was total proof that staying frugal, not wasting things, and saving your money works!

9. I AM THE WARRIOR KID AND I AM A LEADER

If you follow the Warrior Kid Code and are on The Path, guess what? You're not only taking steps to make yourself smarter, stronger, healthier, and better—you're also taking steps to become a leader. How cool is that?!

Being a leader is a big responsibility. REALLY BIG! Uncle Jake always says that just because you're in a position of leadership doesn't automatically make you a GOOD leader. You have to work hard to be a good leader.

Leadership isn't about bossing people around.

It isn't about hogging all the glory and being "number one".

It's about working with others—and sometimes working alone—trying to do what is right.

Sometimes this involves leading a team—like in school, in sports, or in the military. Other times leadership is simply about standing up for what is right in the moment, even when you don't have a team to work with.

One important thing strong leaders and strong Warrior Kids do is they do the right things themselves. This is called leading by example.

TEAMWORK

Leading by example on a team means that as a leader, you are willing to do anything that you expect your teammates to do. A strong leader is willing to do the same hard work that the rest of the team does. Being a leader does not earn you time off from doing the work! In fact, as a leader you should set an example by being the hardest working member of the team!

GO TEAM!

Do you remember when Coach Adam named me the jiu-jitsu team captain at Victory MMA in the third Warrior Kid book? That was a huge honor! Now, ask yourself how you would act if you were the captain—the leader—of your jiu-jitsu class, or any sport you play. Would you be willing to set up the equipment with the rest of your team? Would you dive in and train with everyone during practice? Would you clean up at the end with everybody else—or would you sit back, boss everyone around, and watch them do the "boring" stuff?

You'd be pitching in, of course! Because it's the right thing to do. It's what Warrior Kids do!

STANDING UP FOR WHAT'S RIGHT

There are times when you will have to lead by example all by yourself, without anyone to help you. That can be super intimidating! In these situations, you will lean on everything you've learned through your journey on The Path. *EVERYTHING!*

You will be tested on how level-headed you are. On your sense of fairness. On your judgment. On your resolve. Your self-confidence will be tested. Even your courage!

I'm talking about moments that come out of nowhere, where something wrong is happening. These are situations where other people are being affected and someone needs to step up and lead.

Maybe a bully is picking on a smaller kid in front of you, or someone is cutting the school lunch line and needs to be reminded that their behavior isn't cool. Or maybe you're at the grocery store and someone's grandmother needs help grabbing something off the top shelf or has dropped a bag of groceries and needs a hand. Maybe a friend has failed an important test or is falling off The Path and needs some words of encouragement.

Warrior Kids are always leaders, at any time, and without expecting anything in return except making a positive difference.

When Coach Adam named me team captain of my jiu-jitsu class, I was pumped because I worked REALLY HARD to earn it. But so did Danny Rhinehart and I knew how badly he wanted to be captain. I also knew how much time and effort he sacrificed to make sure his brother Anthony, who had developmental disabilities, always had someone to play with.

I decided to ask Coach Adam to make BOTH Danny and I co-captains! Danny was super qualified and really deserved it. Sure, I could have just accepted my promotion and led our team alone. But I knew we'd be a better team with two of us leading and I knew how much being a co-captain would motivate Danny (and me!). I also knew that the rest of the team would think it was really cool to have two captains. It was the right thing to do. It was also one of my proudest moments as a leader! So cool!

SECTION TWO
DISCIPLINE

Discipline is hard! Being disciplined is hard. If it was easy to be disciplined everyone would be. Discipline is at the heart of being on the Warrior Kid Path and if you want to be a Warrior Kid and be on The Path, you have to work hard and practice discipline.

WHAT DISCIPLINE IS

Discipline comes from within. It comes from YOU. It's about following rules that YOU set for YOURSELF. It's about doing things that are difficult and hard in the moment but that make you stronger, smarter, and better in the long run.

Remember how Kenny Williamson used to tease me and bully me? I'll never forget it! It stunk! The only way I was going to be able to stand up to him and get him to stop bullying me was through discipline. Here's what I started doing.

- I woke up super early every day to work out with Uncle Jake.
- I pushed myself every day to get better at pull-ups and push-ups and burpees to make my body strong.
- I practiced jiu-jitsu—something I had never even heard of before—to learn how to defend myself.
- I stopped eating junk food and started eating healthy foods to fuel my body.
- I read and studied and learned as much as I could, which made me smarter and

grew my self-confidence.

- I went to sleep early to make sure I was rested and able to wake up early so I could GET AFTER IT and train with Uncle Jake the next morning!

Can you imagine how hard it was to stick to ALL of those things... especially in the middle of the summer? HA!! I had planned to play video games, sleep in, eat hot dogs and chips, and drink Mountain Dew the whole time until school started back up!

But playing video games, eating junk food, and being lazy is EASY. All of those things are fun in the moment, but they are a BIG ZERO when it comes to helping you stand up to and defeat a bully like Kenny Williamson! Those things don't help you get stronger, help you get over your fears, or help you get better at things like school, sports, and jiu-jitsu—and they don't help you become a Warrior Kid!

DISCIPLINE EQUALS FREEDOM.
Video games equal ZERO.

HARD WORK

You're going to read this a million times in this Field Manual: being disciplined is hard and it takes tons of hard work be disciplined.

It takes zero effort to be lazy and undisciplined! When you are being lazy, you don't have to do ANYTHING. It's EASY! But there's no reward for being lazy and only doing what's easy. You don't become smarter, stronger, healthier, or better when you're on the easy path.

But Warrior Kids don't take the easy path. They don't cave in to sleeping the day away. They don't stuff themselves with junk food. They don't goof off in class.

Warrior Kids GET AFTER IT!!

Warriors set goals, create rules, and work hard! They push themselves to practice things and face their fears. All of that hard work will pay off—look at how it helped me finally stand up to Kenny! All that hard work earned me freedom from Kenny's bullying.

If you practice discipline, you'll earn freedom from the things that are holding you back as well. Because Discipline Equals Freedom!

THE REWARD OF DISCIPLINE

It can be super tempting to let your mind wander when you're pushing yourself to work hard, stay focused, and maintain discipline. For example: you're studying at home for a tough math test, and you can't stop thinking about how fun it would be to stop studying and just play some video games instead.

Don't do it! Don't let your mind wander onto easy stuff! It's difficult to stop those thoughts but there are other things you can think about to stay focused.

Think about how the hard work you are doing is going to help you get smarter and better. Think about how important math is in the fields of science, technology, architecture, aviation and more! If you're good at math, you're set up to be good at just about anything—you could become a scientist that helps clean up the oceans or an engineer that builds the world's tallest building or an astronaut that steps foot on Mars. How cool is that?!

And this isn't just about math. This is about everything! It's about ALL the things you give your best effort to stay disciplined at.

So, while hard work and discipline may not seem like fun in the moment, it's what will make you a smarter, stronger, healthier, and better Warrior Kid. That is the reward of discipline.

DISCIPLINE EQUALS FREEDOM

Uncle Jake has a lot of awesome sayings like "Detach!", "Bust 'em!" and "Get after it!" My favorite, though, is "Discipline Equals Freedom." It's really simple. By being disciplined you create FREEDOM *FROM* weakness, and you create FREEDOM *TO* do great things.

Here's some of the ways discipline created freedom for me–if you've read all the Way of the Warrior Kid books, you'll recognize them all!

Discipline will not let you down! It gives you the freedom to do the things you want in life!

DISCIPLINE	FREEDOM FROM...	FREEDOM TO...
Practice pull-ups.	Getting teased for not being able to do pull-ups and feeling physically weak.	Be physically fit and confident that I can overcome physical challenges.
Study my times tables.	Always failing math tests and feeling stupid.	Feel smart and confident that I can learn if I apply myself.
Practice jiu-jitsu.	Getting bullied and intimidated by bigger, meaner kids.	Stand up for myself and others and defend myself if necessary.
Repeat visits to the river with Uncle Jake.	Feeling scared of the water and getting teased for not being able to swim.	Go swimming and know that I can face my biggest fears head-on.
Work hard at my lawn mowing business.	Not having money and not being able to buy a new bike.	Learn how to budget my money and be financially independent.
Clean, restore and, rebuild my old bicycle.	Not having a convenient way to get to summer camp.	Understand how to fix things that I have and not waste money.
Train to run a mile in under six minutes.	Being complacent with performing "just good enough."	Understand how to push myself outside my comfort zone.

SELF-DISCIPLINE

Discipline has to come from within. To be a Warrior Kid, to be truly disciplined, you must practice self-discipline. This is when YOU push yourself, when YOU take control and decide to take on the difficult things that come with being a Warrior Kid and staying on The Path. The things you know are the right things to do.

Uncle Jake taught me the difference between *self-discipline* and *imposed discipline*. Imposed discipline is when someone else, like a parent, a teacher, a coach, or someone in a position of authority orders you to do something. They are telling you what to do so you can get better and it can be very helpful. Everyone can use help staying disciplined. But, that type of discipline isn't as strong as self-discipline. Self-discipline comes from YOU. It allows you to make yourself better, to push yourself even harder. True discipline comes from within.

I am the Warrior Kid. I am Discipline.

Imagine if your parents told you that you couldn't play any video games on school nights. You would listen to them, of course, because you're supposed to listen to your parents. But your parents won't always be there to tell you to do the right thing.

Now if YOU decide to be disciplined and not play video games during school nights, without your parents' input, then guess what? It is YOUR DECISION! YOU are in control. You are taking steps to push yourself to be better. Self-discipline is stronger and better because it comes from YOU. AWESOME!!

WILLPOWER

If you had told me that I'd be able to dig deep and find a way to run a mile in less than six minutes during the summer after seventh grade, I'd say you were crazy! Like I mentioned, I'm not naturally a good runner. Also, when Uncle Jake started timing my one-mile runs, I couldn't even run it in less than seven minutes even though I thought I was pushing myself to the limit!

But I wasn't REALLY pushing myself to my limit.

That summer, I learned what pushing myself to the limit was all about. I had to push myself out of my comfort zone... meaning WAY beyond my limits—because my limits were too easy and too comfortable.

Each time I ran, I pushed myself harder than the time before. My entire body would hurt, my lungs burned, and my legs felt like they were going to explode! Despite that discomfort, I pushed.

I needed my mind to be strong. I needed determination. I needed a strong will and willpower. Willpower is when you REFUSE TO GIVE UP. Willpower is when you hear that voice saying you can't do something or you should give up, and you make the decision to NOT LISTEN to that voice and give it your all.

Willpower is like a superpower! With it you can push through difficulties, stay on The Path, and stay disciplined.

WHAT HAPPENS IF YOU GO OFF THE PATH

Sometimes you will find yourself falling off The Path. It happens to every Warrior Kid. And guess what? It's easy to do! Too easy! The problem is that once you do fall off, it's also easy to make excuses to stay off The Path. Once you have a cookie, you can convince yourself that it's okay to have one more, two more, three more, and then you think you might as well have ice cream and donuts too! And once you're that far off The Path, the next day you're skipping pull-ups, jiu-jitsu classes, and the only exercise you're getting is lifting pizza slices to your mouth! Ha! Then you start sleeping in because you feel too sick and lazy!

You don't want that to happen. And it won't happen if you take the right steps.

First off, remember no one is perfect. There's not a single warrior or Warrior Kid out there that is perfect. Even Uncle Jake falls off The Path. How do I know? Because he told me!

Want to know the best thing to do when you fall off?

GET BACK ON IT!

Listen, when you fall off The Path, you may feel mad, sad, or guilty and that's okay. Just detach from those feelings. Lean your head back and take some deep breaths.

This will help you detach and not let your emotions take over.

Also take a moment and think about how crappy it feels to have fallen off The Path. Don't make yourself feel bad—remember you've detached from those feelings. Just think about how falling off The Path does ZERO good for you. Make a promise to never forget that.

Then GET BACK ON THE PATH.

Go do some pull-ups or push-ups. Maybe there's a jiu-jitsu class your parents can drive you to. Or how about grabbing a book and reading it? There are tons of different ways to get yourself back on The Path.

The good news is that whenever you notice you're falling off, you just have to get back on.

MAKE IT FUN!

Just because discipline takes effort and hard work doesn't mean it shouldn't be fun. Warrior Kids are still kids! Kids should have fun! If you find while you're on The Path that you're not having fun, the first thing you should do is ask yourself why?

Maybe it's because what you're doing seems, well... boring. Maybe it seems repetitive. Maybe it seems too easy. Maybe it seems too difficult. Maybe you're too tired or maybe your body is sore. These are all valid reasons. After all, when you're pushing yourself and concentrating a ton it can get pretty serious! It's easy to forget to make it fun.

I've got some ideas to help!

IF THINGS GET BORING OR REPETITIVE

Make a game out of it! Let's say you and your brother or sister have to rake and bag up the leaves in your yard. You could turn it into a race to see who can get the job done faster, or who can stuff the most bags.

Do things in a completely different way than you've ever done before! Imagine you're folding the laundry. Folding piece after piece... you could try and sing a song while you're doing it—singing about each piece of clothing as you fold them! You can get really creative and probably crack yourself up!

Let's imagine you're cleaning your room for the MILLIONTH TIME! Try picking up and putting things away in alphabetical order, or by color. Pick your favorite color first and just pick up things that are that color. Then go through all the colors, one at a time.

Nothing makes Discipline more fun than a bunch of clowns. Am I right, Marc?

I don't think the Warrior Kid Code mentions clowns...

IF THINGS ARE TOO EASY

Make things more challenging! Maybe you're setting the table for dinner for the BIL-LIONTH TIME. You could try and see if you can place all the silverware exactly where each piece is supposed to go—but with your eyes closed! That's not so easy!

Maybe at jiu-jitsu class the kids you're training with aren't pushing you hard enough. Then ask your coach to match you up with the more experienced kids who can really take your skills to another level!

Maybe you're able to do fifty pull-ups in record time. Well, try doing them with your legs and feet pointed out in front of you so your body is shaped like a giant "L"!

WIN OR LEARN

Let's imagine you're being REALLY disciplined and working hard at reaching a goal. Like doing twenty pull-ups or getting an A on a test at school or winning on the mat that week at jiu-jitsu. And let's imagine that you FAIL to reach the goal you've set for yourself. When this happens do not get mad. Do not get upset. Remember Warrior Kid Code #7: *The Warrior Kid stays humble, controls his ego, and stays calm. Warrior Kids do not lose their tempers.*

It is perfectly fine to fail. Warriors fail all the time! It's what warriors do with failure that sets them apart! They look at why they failed and LEARN FROM IT so they can become better.

So, keep a calm head and think about why you failed. Maybe you couldn't reach your pull-up goal because you weren't eating healthy enough and your muscles weren't properly fueled. Maybe you didn't reach your goal on a school test because you went to bed too late the night before and were too tired to concentrate. And maybe you got submitted at jiu-jitsu because your opponent simply knew moves and submissions you didn't even know existed! I've actually had to deal with these exact failures! So has Uncle Jake!

There's a big difference between failing and losing. If you can apply what you learned from failure, you actually never lose. Uncle Jake always says "Win or Learn," which means you either succeed at your goal or you *learn* from failing to reach it. The only way you lose is if you're not disciplined in how you react to failure. Just stay calm, learn from the situation, and apply those learnings to what you do going forward.

I failed a LOT when I first started jiu-jitsu. But every failure was an opportunity to learn!

FLASHBACK FROM:

WAY ᴼᶠ ᴛʜᴇ WARRIOR KID
FROM WIMPY TO WARRIOR THE NAVY SEAL WAY

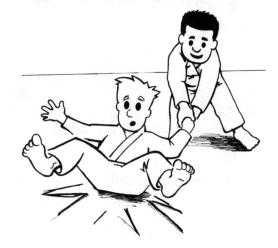

DISCIPLINE ACTIVITIES

There are tons of ways to be disciplined. Warrior Kids try and be disciplined as much as they can throughout the day. Here are some examples. Can you think of other ways to practice discipline?

- Getting up early.
- Avoiding too many 'lazy day activities' like eating junk food, playing video games, or watching TV.
- Exercising.
- Cleaning your room.
- Helping out with household chores.
- Paying attention in class and not fooling around.
- Checking the Warrior Kid Code throughout the day to make sure you're staying on The Path.
- Making a to-do list of important things you want to do and checking them off.
- Eating healthy.
- Training at martial arts.
- Doing your homework in a timely manner.
- Saving your money.
- Reading a book or a magazine.
- Writing.
- Learning how to play a musical instrument.
- Drawing and coloring, and painting.
- Going to sleep early.

THE RIGHT THING

"The right thing." I've mentioned that, like, a million times already in this Field Manual! But do you know what it *really* means? Have your parents ever told you exactly what the "right thing" is? What about your teachers or friends? I'm asking because it's actually a super important concept. It's at the core of the Warrior Kid Code and our journeys on the Warrior Kid Path.

Uncle Jake helped me understand that deep inside each of us Warrior Kids, regular kids, pretty much EVERYONE—there is a universal understanding of what the "right thing" and "*doing* the right thing" means:

It's about being a good person as much as you can in everything that you do.

It means being good and kind to other people and it means being good and kind to yourself.

It's about knowing the difference between right and wrong and having the discipline to choose to DO RIGHT even if it is harder, takes more effort, and might not be as easy as DOING WRONG.

Pretty intense, right? Yeah, but nothing us Warrior Kids can't handle!

PARENTS AND ADULTS

Parents, grandparents, aunts, uncles, or whatever adults we live with are ALWAYS telling us what to do. "Pay attention! Clean your room! Pick up your mess! Set the table!

Make your bed! Fix your hair! Because I said so! Leave your sister alone! Leave your brother alone! Turn off the TV! No more video games! Brush your teeth! Get to bed... !"

Sound familiar? Haha, I bet it does!

I know adults can seem like their whole purpose is to find ways to become annoyed with us. But the reason they tell us to do all this stuff and stick their nose in our business is because they CARE. They are actually trying to raise us and teach us how to be good people and how to do the right thing. They want to show us how to be strong and fair and to be able to do great things with our lives.

Uncle Jake has helped me understand what it means to do the right thing.

We really shouldn't give them a hard time about it. It's not easy, but it's the right thing.

Think about it. They've already been kids and they had parents and adults that taught them the difference between right and wrong. Plus, they've been adults for a while and all that experience has taught them so much more about life than us kids know yet!

They work at their jobs and spend their hard-earned money to give us kids a good life—whether they have a lot of money or very little. My dad is hardly around because he has to travel for long periods of time for his job. He does that to support my mom and me. My mom also works for the same reasons and she has to deal with ME all the time. I bet if you asked her, she'd tell you it's not easy!

No one cares about you succeeding in life as much as your parents or the adults in your family. A true Warrior Kid understands this and works hard to show that they understand.

Here is one last thing to remember—and it is one of the hardest things about life as a kid. Remember that adults aren't perfect. They make mistakes. They might lose their temper. They might not do the right thing. They might eat junk food or not exercise. They might even do things that hurt you or your family. If something like that happens, learn from it. Learn what not to do. Learn not to act that way. When you see adults do something wrong, remember that you are on a path to do the right thing and become a better person, regardless of what anyone else does.

HOW TO KNOW YOU'RE DOING THE RIGHT THING

A great way to help you figure out how to do the right thing is to follow a code. Just like I created the Warrior Kid Code, you can create one that fits your life and the things you think you should do that are RIGHT.

And do you know what to do with that code? Hang it up where you know you will see it every day! That could be your bedroom wall, door, the refrigerator, on your notebooks, in your school locker—or all of those places! The more you see it, the more you'll remember it and that means the better you'll be at knowing what the right thing to do is in any situation.

My Warrior Kid Code is hung up right on my bedroom door!

ASK YOURSELF THIS...

You're going to find yourself in situations where you're just not sure what the right thing to do is and you don't have a lot of time to react. I know because I've been in these situations—even with my Warrior Kid Code burned into my brain—where I'm not sure what to do!

I have a simple solution that's pretty foolproof. I ask myself, "What would my parents and Uncle Jake think of my decision? Would they be disappointed or proud of me?"

Here's an example for you:

Let's just say you have a SUPER important social studies test tomorrow to study for. You've just finished dinner and there's an AWESOME TV show on that all your friends are going to be watching and talking about the next day at school. You know you need to study but also you REALLY want to watch that show and be in on the fun with your friends. Well, just ask yourself what your parents would think if you had to explain any of these decisions that you could make:

1. Watch the TV show and don't study. Sure, you'll probably do a TERRIBLE JOB on the math test but talking about the show with your friends is going to be the BEST!

2. Study WHILE watching the TV show. Sure, you'll barely be able to study but at least you'll be in on all the cool gossip and jokes with your friends tomorrow at school! Fingers crossed you pass the test!

3. Study! That TV show does absolutely nothing for you! When your friends are hanging out talking about the show you can still hang with them—but with the

the confidence and PRIDE that you gave your best effort on the test.

So... which choice do you think your parents would be proud of? I know which one Uncle Jake and my parents would be proud of. If you're honest with yourself, you'll know the right thing to do is skip the TV show, study hard, and ACE THAT TEST!

HONESTY

Everyone makes mistakes and it's easy sometimes to think that when you make them that you're ALWAYS going to get in trouble for them. I get it. But it's not actually true. YES, you're going to get an earful most of the time when you make a mistake but that's actually okay. Remember all the mistakes I made during my fifth grade, sixth grade, and seventh grade? I was the world champion of mistake-making!

Now, there are times when you're going to be tempted to lie and cover up the fact that you made a mistake. Maybe it's your parents, a sibling, a friend, or a teacher that you really don't want to get mad at you or make fun of you or judge you.

But it would be absolutely WRONG to lie and cover up your mistake. No matter what the mistake is.

Maybe you break a glass while clearing the dinner table. Or maybe you were teasing your younger brother and made him cry. Maybe you stayed too long at your friend's house and got home late for dinner. Whatever the situation—Warrior Kids admit when they've made a mistake and learn from them.

Learning helps you become smarter and better so you won't make that mistake again. All it takes is looking back on what you did that led to the mistake. Were you rushing to clear the dinner table super-fast so you could watch TV? Were you teasing your younger brother because you're jealous of the attention he gets from your parents? Did you stay too long at your friend's house because you convinced yourself that nobody would mind if you arrived late for dinner? I'm guilty of that one!

But guess what? The more you take responsibility for your mistakes and show that you're learning from them, the more people will trust and believe in you and the less they'll get mad.

Want to know what's really bad? Lying and then getting caught. Lying takes your mistake and makes it about a million times worse! And it makes everyone super disappointed and mad at you—which is what you wanted to avoid to begin with!

HELPING OTHERS

Warrior Kids are leaders and leaders help other people out all the time. In fact, people often look to leaders for help, guidance, and answers, which means you need to be prepared to give help, guidance, and answers to those that need them! It's the right thing to do!

You may be scratching your head right now and thinking, "Marc, who could possibly need my help, guidance, and answers? I'm just a kid!" Well the excuse "I'm just a kid!" doesn't cut it—because you're not just a kid. You're a Warrior Kid.

Think about it. Everyone could use your help. And you know what's totally awesome about helping people out? You make them feel good and making them feel good will make you feel good. Total bonus!

I made a really cool chart that has some pretty obvious ways you can help out. Maybe you are already doing some—maybe you could do even more!

WHO	WAYS YOU SHOULD HELP THEM OUT
Parents and Adults	• Do your household chores like clean your room, make your bed, take out the garbage, and set and clear the dinner table. • Look after your brothers and sisters. • Walk and feed the family pet. • Offer to make your own school lunches. • Ask them regularly "Hey can I help you with anything?" • Avoid complaining if you don't get your way and keep a positive attitude.
Teachers	• Show up to class prepared and with your homework done. • Pay attention to the teacher and don't cause distractions. • Ask questions if you don't understand something. • Offer to help clean the chalkboards or put away books. • Help out your fellow students.
Friends	• Team up to study for school tests and help each other to do homework. • Encourage them to get on the Warrior Kid Path and follow The Code. • Always act supportive if they're going through a hard time. • If they're sick, offer to help them and their family out with their chores. • If they're less fortunate than you, share your lunch, give them toys or clothes that your parents agree you no longer need.

COMPUTERS

Computers are SUPER COOL! They're pretty much the ultimate weapon when it comes to learning at school and doing your homework. Uncle Jake told me the computers he used when he was a kid were not even close to the ones we have now!

So, yeah, computers are awesome for education. BUT—they can also be super distracting because of all the games, videos, GIFs, memes, and social media stuff. Uncle Jake warned me that computers can become a big black hole of meaningless junk—and he's right! Some kids I know play video games and watch videos nonstop, all day and all night! Then they're exhausted the next day for school and, if it's a weekend, they sleep in and waste the day. Then they start all over again with that black hole of meaningless junk! Yuck!

That's what I call doing the WRONG THING!

Do you remember when Uncle Jake told me that time was precious at the end of my seventh grade summer? Well, I remember! In fact, I'll never forget what he said. NO ONE gets a second chance with life which means we never get back the time we waste on things like computer games, goofy cat videos, social media, and LAZY DAYS! That's lost time that you could be spending doing the right thing, doing something REAL... like practicing jiu-jitsu, exercising, doing important chores, or hanging out with your friends—doing the right things and LEARNING.

VIDEO GAMES AND TV

I bet you can guess what I'm going to say about video games and TV after what I just said about computers!

That's right! They're a black hole of NOTHING! Wait... do you know what a black hole is? A black hole is an object in space where the gravity is so strong that nothing can escape from it. NOTHING! Even light gets sucked into a black hole. That's what happens to your time and your brain when you use computers for games and meaningless videos.

I wasted so many days on video games before I got on The Path.

FLASHBACK FROM:
WAY ᴼᶠ ᴛʜᴇ WARRIOR KID
THE COLORING BOOK!

I know… I know… they're both super fun. It can seem like the best time when you and your friends are pitted against each other, shooting it up, racing around and crushing high scores—or crushing potato chips while binge-watching TV for hours! But think about it… what are computer games and videos actually doing for you? They aren't getting you better at anything REAL. They don't make you smarter, stronger, healthier, or better. They make you dumber, weaker, and less healthy!

Uncle Jake told me that the people that make computer games and videos actually design them to be addicting, so you just want to keep wasting time with them. I think he's right! It's super hard to stop playing them because you always want to try and go farther, get a higher score, or watch another episode! That's why when your mom tells you to turn the computer game or the TV off, you don't want to! That's not being on The Path—that's jumping into a black hole! Warrior Kids have the inner strength and discipline to do bigger and better things and not waste their time on lazy days and junk!

JUNK FOOD

I think I've already made it clear how much I loved junk food! But once I accepted how bad that garbage was for me... how sick it made me... how it weak it made me... it was easy to give it up.

Well... not that easy! HA!

It's actually super hard in the beginning to stop eating all those sugary junk foods! But we know that a Warrior Kid doesn't avoid hard things. A Warrior Kid faces them head on and comes out smarter, stronger, healthier, and better!

So, do the right thing, stay disciplined, and stick to healthy, real foods!

You can totally do it! REMEMBER, just like how online videos, social media, computer games, and TV offer you NOTHING REAL, junk food does the same thing! Wasting time on things that offer you nothing and rob you of your precious time and strength is the opposite of doing the right thing.

Truly being on The Path means eating healthy, feeding your brain to be sharp and fueling your body to be strong—Warrior Kid strong!

REWARDS

Are you getting sick of all this talk about the *right thing*? Are you thinking, "C'mon, Marc, being a Warrior Kid sounds like ZERO fun! I CAN'T mess around on the computer! I CAN'T play video games! I CAN'T watch funny videos online! I CAN'T even eat french fries!!!! What kind of kid doesn't eat french fries?!"

I totally get it.

First off, being a Warrior Kid IS FUN and TOTALLY AWESOME—but for a different reason. Pushing yourself so that you get smarter, stronger, healthier, and better feels GREAT! Since I've been on The Path, I've gone from ZERO push-ups to more than I can even count! I'm a MILLION times better at school, I've become captain of my jiu-jitsu class, I can now run a mile in less than six minutes, and here I am ACTUALLY WRITING MY OWN BOOK!

It's all fun because I earned it! I have tons of fun with my friends because we all support each other and push each other. IT'S SO AWESOME!

And guess what? When I achieve a really difficult goal—like acing a major test, setting a personal best for pull-ups, or winning a jiu-jitsu tournament against a REALLY tough opponent—I *reward* myself. Sometimes that means I let myself have a cheeseburger. I've had a bunch with Uncle Jake at the Olde Malt Shoppe! Sometimes I'll play a few video games with my friends. I might watch movies with my parents. And YES I DO EAT FRENCH FRIES! I mean, c'mon, how can I eat a cheeseburger and not have fries? After all, I'm a Warrior KID, not a Warrior Robot!

But here's the thing. I only do these things occasionally and as a reward for *after* I've EARNED THEM! By EARNING the reward, the occasional video game, maybe a slice of pizza, or a mint chocolate chip milkshake doesn't become a black hole of NOTHING! These things can be good when they have a purpose—as a REWARD for doing something AWESOME as a Warrior Kid!

This Warrior Robot doesn't have to worry about caving in to junk food!

Actually. Human. I. _____ Sometimes. Reward. Myself. With. Snacks. Of. Old. Coins. And. Used. Motor. Oil.

When you EARN the reward, they are even better. And then, after the reward, you GET BACK ON THE PATH and start earning your next reward.

See how that works?! AWESOME!

PEER PRESSURE

There are going to be times when your friends or other kids—your peers—are going to put PRESSURE on you to do something they want you to do. This could be something really cool, like pressuring you to do as many push-ups as they can or motivating you to help someone with a tough job. This is positive peer pressure.

But other times they might be pressuring you to do something bad—or something that you know is WRONG. Maybe they're daring you to cut class, lie to your parents, to steal something from a store, or curse and use swear words when you talk. This is negative peer pressure.

It's SUPER important to stay on The Path and do what is right and not give in to negative peer pressure. It can seem tough because it's natural to want to fit in with your friends and with other kids—to "follow along"—but Warrior Kids don't follow. They LEAD.

You might get teased—I've actually had kids make fun of me and call me a wimp for not doing something I knew was wrong! Ha! I've also had kids tell me that doing something wrong will make me look cool and tough. Are you kidding me?! No way! If this happens to you, don't believe them! You're actually being strong—Warrior Kid strong—for standing up, doing the right thing, and not giving into negative peer pressure!

TROUBLEMAKING FRIENDS

We all have those friends whom we like but for one reason or another they always seem to be causing trouble. It's like they LOVE to cause problems and create chaos—and somehow, whenever you're hanging out with them, you're getting caught up in the chaos as well! Maybe they crack jokes when the teacher is trying to teach or they're cutting in line during lunch and trying to drag you along or maybe they make fun of other kids.

Well, let me tell you something, when you go along with someone like that you are actually letting them LEAD YOU in the WRONG direction. You need to LEAD THEM in the RIGHT direction.

We *MAY* have been troublemakers before we got on The Path. Right Kenny?

My lawyer recommends I not comment on the matter...

First step: tell them that they shouldn't be doing what they're doing. DON'T get mad. DON'T talk down to them. DON'T act like you're better than them. You never know what is going on in their lives. You can ask them nicely why they're acting like a troublemaker.

Maybe they're acting out for attention. Maybe their younger brothers or sisters get all the attention at home so they have to cause trouble to get attention from their family—and they think that it's okay to do the same at school. Maybe their home life is chaos and so chaos is the only situation they feel comfortable with!

Maybe they don't know. Maybe they don't care. Maybe they just love to cause chaos... well, then you need to take steps to get away from the chaos they create. You may need to tell them you can't hang out with them. I know that stinks! It's hard to tell someone that! But you need to always be a leader, not just for them, but for yourself.

Lead by example and stay out of the chaos and away from their troublemaking. Hopefully with time, they will finally see how awesome it is to be on The Path and get on it themselves.

SECTION FOUR
'BUST EM!'

NEWS FLASH! Warrior Kids work hard to be physically strong and fit! Oh, you already knew that?!! Hahaha! But seriously, this means we do lots of exercise, physical activity, and sports. That way when we need to "Get after it!" or "Bust em!" or "Get some!", we're ready!

Before I got on The Path, I wasn't strong. I wasn't confident and I absolutely was not a warrior! Back during the summer after fifth grade, one of the first things Uncle Jake and I worked on was getting my body strong. It took hard work, patience, discipline, and repetition. It's something I still work hard at every single day—and so should you!

You know what's awesome about getting after it through exercise, sports, and martial arts? It makes you stronger in tons of ways:

- Makes you a stronger leader.
- Makes your brain stronger.
- Gives you more confidence.
- Improves your humility.
- Improves your problem solving.
- Helps you make awesome friends.
- Creates a powerful sense of "team."

Uncle Jake told me that getting physically stronger is a lifelong effort! At first I was like, *WHAAAAAT*?! But now it totally makes sense. When I did my first pull-up, I thought I had accomplished so much–but then I got stronger and was able to do ten and I thought THAT was a lot! Then I got even stronger and was able to do twenty... Now I can do TONS more and in the near future, I bet you I can do even more than I can today–as long as I keep at it!

Uncle Jake always tells me that the stronger we get now, the stronger we'll be when we get older... and warriors need to focus on getting stronger so that we're always prepared for whatever happens–whether we're eight of sixty-eight!

EXERCISING AND SPORTS

Exercising and playing sports are your best weapons for getting physically stronger, and each one makes you better at the other. There are tons of exercises you can do and tons of sports you can play–which is awesome because you can try them all and find out which ones you like, which ones you're good at, and which ones you need to get better at!

In section seven of this book, you'll find some cool exercises any Warrior Kid can do!

REPETITIONS AND SETS

There are a couple of exercise terms I learned from Uncle Jake that you should know:

- A rep: This means repetitions. It's just how many times you can an exercise in a row without stopping. So if you can do twenty pull-ups before you need to stop and take a break, you've done twenty REPS of pull-ups.

- A set: A set describes each grouping of reps you do. For example, if you did twenty reps of push-ups and took a break, then did another twenty push-ups and took a break, then did twenty more push-ups... you just did three SETS of push-ups.

Hey, Nora, I'm on my fifth set of ten!!

Nice. I did six sets of twelve this morning. Keep working!

KEEPING TRACK

You want to do as many reps in a row, of one exercise until you *really* can't do any more. When you take your break before your next set, write down how many reps you did in that set. Maybe it's five or maybe it's ten. Just write it down, then get back after it for your next set of reps! I like to do five sets for any one exercise.

You're probably wondering why I'm telling you to write down how many reps and sets you did of a particular exercise. Well, you want to get stronger and better right? By keeping track, you're able to compare how many sets and reps you did the week before, the month before—maybe even a year before—and see how much you've improved over time!

JULY 6 EXERCISE	REPS	REPS	REPS	REPS	REPS
Pull Ups	10	10	8	6	4
Burpees	15	15	13	10	7
Sit Ups	15	13	10	8	6
Dips	10	7	6	4	2

CHANGING IT UP

I like to do a different exercise for each day of the week if I can. I'll do sets of push-ups one day, then burpees the next, followed by sit-ups the next day—and of course I'm doing pull-ups at least once or twice a week!

There are a lot of good reasons for changing up your exercise routine:

- There isn't one exercise that works out every muscle in your body, so by changing it up and doing different exercises on different days, you're making sure your exercise routine is balanced and your entire body is getting stronger.
- Doing one exercise all the time is going to get boring pretty quickly, so changing up your routine will keep it fun!
- By doing lots of different exercises, you're going to find out which ones you're naturally good at and which ones you're not—everyone is different when it comes to being good or not so good at things. By changing it up, you're actually making sure you do those exercises you're not as good at and you'll get better at them! How awesome is that?!

PULL-UPS

Speaking of awesome, do you know what's so awesome about pull-ups?

THEY'RE AWESOME! THATS WHAT'S AWESOME ABOUT PULL-UPS!!

They're totally my favorite exercise! Maybe that's because they're the first exercise I actually WORKED HARD AT and PRACTICED and PUSHED MYSELF to get better at with

Uncle Jake. Or maybe it's because they're actually one of the best exercises Warrior Kids can do to get stronger.

You use your arms, shoulders, chest, your back muscles. AND you can add in other movements while you're doing pull-ups to also use your stomach and leg muscles—pretty awesome!

MUSCLES USED FOR PULL-UPS

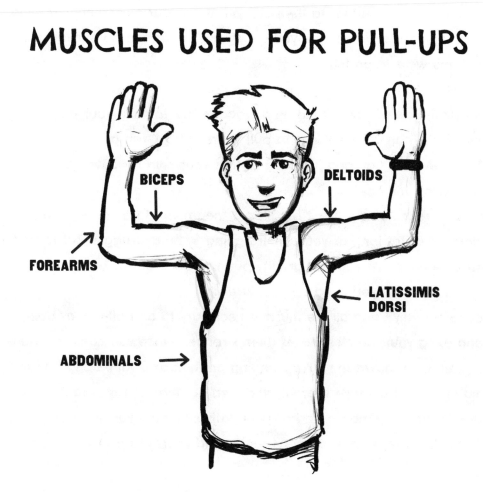

BICEPS

DELTOIDS

FOREARMS

LATISSIMIS DORSI

ABDOMINALS

LEARNING PULL-UPS

So, even though I said pull-ups were AWESOME, they are DEFINITELY NOT easy, which means if you've never done a pull-up or never been good at doing them, it's going to take some hard work. But the good news is: you're a Warrior Kid, you aren't afraid of hard work!

If you can't pull yourself up to the pull-up bar on your own, then you need a way to help build up your strength until you get strong enough to do one. Here are two really awesome ways to do that!

1. Box Assist with a negative: Stand on a wooden box to raise yourself up closer to the bar so you can use your legs to pull yourself up. Grab onto the bar, tell yourself, "I'm a Warrior Kid!" and jump up so that your chin is above the bar and your feet are up off the box.

   Now here's the hard part—it is called a "negative." To do a negative, try and hold yourself up as long as you can. It's going to be a struggle! But resist gravity as best as you can! As you feel gravity pull you back down, keep resisting! Why? Because that is how you build up your strength!

   You're actually using all the muscles necessary to do pull-ups by doing a negative and using your muscles makes them stronger. Once you can't resist any more, let yourself lower down so you're standing on the box again. Congratulations! You just did one rep! Now take a break and then do another rep—exactly what you just did—use the box to jump up and do a negative, holding yourself for as long as you can. Keep doing reps until you can't really hold yourself up at all.

In a few days or a week, you might be able to increase those reps as you get stronger. Soon, you might not need the box at all because you've gotten strong enough to pull yourself up without needing to jump up!

Even I had to use a box when I first learned how to do pull-ups.

FLASHBACK FROM:
WAY OF THE WARRIOR KID
THE COLORING BOOK!

2. Parent Assist: Another way to do pretty much the same thing as the box assist is to have your dad, your mom, or another adult (or maybe an older sibling if you have one) lift you up to the bar. Once you're holding on to it and your chin is level with the bar, they'll gently let go of you so that you can do a negative, holding yourself

up as long as you can.

This is a great way to get strong and do some cool stuff with your family! AWE-SOME!

GETTING BETTER AT PULL-UPS

Like Uncle Jake says, the real key to getting better at pull-ups is... DOING PULL-UPS!

But don't expect to become a pull-up warrior overnight! You're totally going to get stronger each time you do them, but it can take a while to get better and not everyone gets stronger at the same pace. Sometimes, it takes a long time to get stronger—so long that you will barely notice that it is happening. But it will happen over time.

The key is that when you do them—push yourself! But that doesn't mean go crazy! Uncle Jake taught me to stay in control and exercise properly to get *stronger*—not to get *injured*!

Just try and push yourself each time you do pull-ups to do a little bit more than the last time you did them. Maybe it's one or two more reps than last time—or maybe it's doing a fifth set of reps where before you could only do four.

Taking a break for a minute or two between sets is super important to giving your body short rests so it learns to recharge quickly and be ready for your next set of reps.

You WILL get stronger and better at pull-ups with consistent practice, repetition, hard work, eating right, and giving your body a rest when it needs it!

And guess what? This approach to getting better at pull-ups goes for EVERY exercise! If you want to get better at burpees—do more burpees! If you want to get better at push-ups—do more push-ups! Just make sure you keep track of how many you're able to do and when you're pushing yourself make sure you use correct form and are exercising properly.

PULL-UP ADD-ONS

If you get really good at pull-ups—congratulations! That's awesome! That means you've probably done tons of pull-ups. That also means that maybe you might be getting bored of doing the same exercise over and over. Well, if that's the case you need to mix it up! You can add some cool moves to your pull-up routine:

1. Chin-up grip: These are just like pull-ups, but you grip the bar with your hand rotated so that your palms face you and the back of your hands face out away from your body.

2. Wide grip and narrow grip: Just like it sounds! Try alternating so your hands are super far apart for one set and then the next set you put your hands close together on the bar.

3. Tucks: Just like a normal pull-up, but first you raise your knees up and try to tuck them as close to your chest as you can. This type of pull-up is harder than a regular one.

4. L-sit: These are kind of like tucks, but before you do your pull-up, you lift and extend your legs so that your feet are pointing straight out and your body is shaped like an "L."

5. Cliff hangers: Grab the pull-up bar like a baseball bat but with your hands about 6-12 inches apart, then try to lift your body up to the bar. You'll be pulling yourself up, kind of sideways, but it's AWESOME for making your arms and body stronger!

L-SIT

TUCKS

CHIN-UP GRIP

WIDE GRIP

CLIFF HANGERS

SPORTS: PLAY AS MANY AS YOU CAN

Just like every exercise works different parts of your body, every sport helps you develop different physical and mental skills, which means you should play as many as you can! Sure there will be sports you're really good at, ones you're okay at, and ones you stink at! Ha! But that's okay—I stunk at a bunch of sports when I first tried them.

Uncle Jake always reminds me that no one is awesome at everything. We all have stuff we're naturally good at that comes easily to us, and then there's all the stuff we aren't good at that we have to *work hard* to be better at. If we only did things we were good at—or thought we were good at—we wouldn't really be doing much of anything. We would be lazy and lazy is not the Warrior Kid way!

Plus, there are going to be sports you think you're no good at, but once you try them, you'll see you're actually good at them! Remember how bad I was at jiu-jitsu when I started? Two years later I was winning first place medals at tournaments!

GETTING BETTER AT SPORTS

Getting better at sports is just like getting better at pull-ups, math, or anything else. It's going to take practice, repetition, patience, hard work, ego control, and smarts—plus a ton of other things. Sounds like A LOT, right?! But guess what? If sports pushes you to do ALL those things, then sports actually helps you to become a Warrior Kid—because all those things are what makes a Warrior Kid a Warrior Kid!

NOT THE STRONGEST. NOT THE FASTEST

Uncle Jake told me that when he played sports in school, he was never the strongest or the fastest, especially at soccer. So he had to figure out other ways to help out the team. He decided he could help out by being a leader. He would help organize some of the practices. He would lead the other kids in doing exercises and conditioning. Sometimes he'd make sure that the kids on the team got along with each other. He wasn't a star, but he was able to help the team win by figuring out what he was good at.

You can tell what Uncle Jake is good at just by looking at his hands...
HARD WORK!

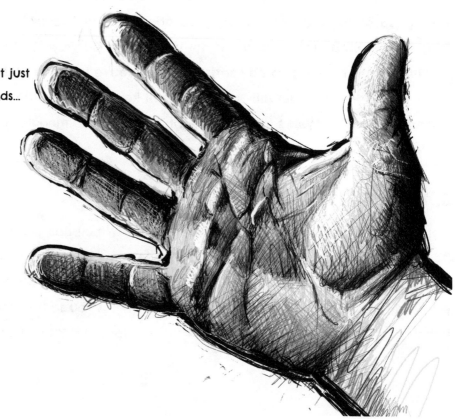

That's pretty awesome! Some kids get mad or sad if they can't be the star. Some kids will decide it's not worth playing if they aren't the fastest or the strongest. Listen, we can't expect to be the best at everything we try! It's impossible. NO ONE can be the best at everything. But we can TRY OUR BEST at everything.

That's what Uncle Jake did. He realized he needed to figure out what he could do to help out the team. It's a team sport! It's not a "ME" sport. He played a key role in the soccer team winning because he was being a team player.

TEAM PLAYER

In many sports, you are going to be part of a team. There will be the team you play on and teams you compete against. This means you're going to meet a lot of new kids on those teams, which means making a lot of great friends and learning all sorts of cool stuff.

- It also means that everyone on your team—especially you—needs to be a TEAM player.
- Being a team player means you always put the team FIRST and always try your best even if you're not the most talented.
- Being a team player means you control your ego and stay humble whether you perform well or not. Warrior Kids don't brag or celebrate when they perform well and don't complain or make excuses when they perform poorly.
- Being a team player means you always support and praise your fellow teammates.

You never put down another teammate or blame them if their performance wasn't their best.

- Being a team player means focusing on the sport, trying to win, and doing your best, not joking around or distracting your teammates from doing their best.
- Being a team player means you win as a team or you learn as a team. No one kid's performance is responsible for a win or for a loss.
- Being a team player means you always respect your opponent and are gracious in victory or defeat.

LOSING

Warriors want to win. That's a good thing! Wanting to win means you're competitive and that means you try to be your best when you compete against other kids. It means you want to push yourself. It means you want to improve all the time.

But how you act when you don't win is also super important. Getting upset, frustrated, or mad when you lose is definitely not good. The more frustrated you get, the more you will actually lose! You'll be too worried about losing instead of focusing on how to do your best.

If you show your frustration when you lose, then everyone is going to think you're a bad sport. No one likes a bad sport AND no one wants to compete against a bad sport.

Losing is also a good thing! It's an opportunity to learn. Again, that's why Uncle Jake always tells me when you compete, you either *WIN or you LEARN*. You can study why you lost, what your opponent did that helped them defeat you, and what you need to work on to help you and your team get better.

For example, one reason Danny Rhinehart was able to use an omoplata to submit me in jiu-jitsu, was because I didn't know the move at all—which meant I couldn't defend against it!

Danny and I were super competitive, but when I asked him about the move, he was happy to share how he did it. And I shared with him a move I used to submit him—the loop choke. And you know what? Later that summer, in a jiu-jitsu tournament, we were able to use what we had learned from losing against each other to beat our toughest opponents! How awesome is that?!

Always treat your opponent with respect. They're actually helping you improve.

FLASHBACK FROM:
WAY OF THE WARRIOR KID
FROM WIMPY TO WARRIOR THE NAVY SEAL WAY

JIU-JITSU AND THE MARTIAL ARTS

Now we've gotten to the REALLY GOOD stuff! Can you guess why jiu-jitsu is awesome? BECAUSE IT'S AWESOME!!

Seriously, jiu-jitsu is one of the most important activities us Warrior Kids can do, right next to pull-ups! While I really like jiu-jitsu, you might like another type of martial arts. You should try a few and see which ones you like the most and which ones have classes that you can easily go to. Here are a few examples but there are tons more you can discover on your own!

- Jiu-jitsu, wrestling, judo, and sambo: These focus on grappling—which means controlling your opponent through position and leverage, much of which takes place on the ground. In jiu-jitsu, judo, and sambo, you can also use position and leverage to make your opponent "tap-out," which means they give up or submit.

- Boxing, kickboxing and Muay Thai: These focus on striking—which means hitting an opponent with punches, knees, kicks, and elbows while trying not to get hit yourself!

- MMA or "mixed martial arts": Mixed martial arts is exactly what it sounds like. It teaches you to combine or mix different techniques from different martial arts. If you've ever heard of the UFC—the Ultimate Fighting Championship—the athletes in that league practice mixed martial arts.

WHY JIU-JITSU

One of the best things about jiu-jitsu is that it pushes you in tons of ways that make you a smarter, stronger, healthier, and better Warrior Kid!

Practicing jiu-jitsu is like being part of the greatest club in the world!

Here are some ways jiu-jitsu helps:

- It helps you develop both your body and mind because you're using both all the time.
- Your body will become stronger, more flexible, and your reflexes will get quicker.
- You'll develop your mental creativity to figure out how to counter your opponent's moves and think up moves to try on them.
- Every move you make in jiu-jitsu is connected to all the other moves, which helps your ability to strategize and think about the big picture—meaning every move, not just one!
- Jiu-jitsu shows you how much discipline and hard work pays off and helps you get better.
- It builds self-confidence as you get better and teaches you how to defend yourself against an opponent.
- Jiu-jitsu teaches humility and sportsmanship because you will win or LEARN each time you train with your opponent.
- Jiu-jitsu gives you some of the most awesome friends in the world!

STARTING AT JIU-JITSU

FIRST THING: jiu-jitsu is not just a sport or a game. It is a martial art that can be dangerous if you do it wrong. Chokes, armlocks, and other techniques can REALLY HURT people if they are done wrong. So don't ever train jiu-jitsu without a coach or an adult around, especially when you first start training jiu-jitsu.

If you're new to jiu-jitsu, you'll probably be nervous when you first show up to your jiu-jitsu academy. It's intimidating to see a bunch of kids grappling, pushing each other, and rolling around on mats on the floor. And then having to join in WITH NO EXPERIENCE? Ha! But trust me, it's SO AWESOME!

Like I've said before—everyone in every jiu-jitsu class has had to go through their first day—and they're *still* learning tons of new stuff all the time even though they've been doing it for a while. This means the kids who have a lot more experience than you can appreciate the fact that you're just learning because they're "just learning" too—they've just been learning it for longer.

To learn, all you have to do is listen. And watch. And ask. And try your best. Your jiu-jitsu instructor is going to be an awesome help! They're there to make sure every-one is practicing safely and fairly and learning. And all those kids in your class? They can teach you tons of stuff, too!

HOW OFTEN

Realistically, it's going to take you about six months of going to jiu-jitsu class before you feel like you "get it". If you really want to get better, you should train at LEAST twice a week. If you only go once a week, you might forget what you've learned the week before. Now, if you REALLY want to improve, you could go three times a week! Even if you can't go to jiu-jitsu as often as you want, you can think about the moves so you remember them. I've even known kids that practice the moves on pillows or stuffed animals!

I don't know if I can take him... that blank, cold stare. He doesn't even look scared of me...!

UNIFORM

Jiu-jitsu has a traditional uniform called the "gi." Gis are made up of loose, drawstring pants and a long jacket that wraps around your waist and stays closed with a belt. They're really thick and durable so that they hold up to the stress of jiu-jitsu. Your belt not only keeps your gi shut, it also represents what rank you are as a jiu-jitsu martial artist. Beginners start with a white belt and experts get a black belt—with a bunch of color combos in between that you earn as you get better. Pretty cool, right?!

The other cool thing about gis is that when you roll with an opponent, you can totally use their gi as part of your defense or offense by grabbing, twisting, and holding on to it. Just remember: your opponent can do the same with yours!

You won't always use a gi to do jiu-jitsu. Sometimes you will train without the gi—something that is called "no-gi." That makes sense, right?!? When you don't wear a gi, you just wear shorts and a t-shirt or what's called a rash-guard, which is a tight shirt that doesn't get caught up in your opponent's fingers or toes.

FLASHBACK FROM:
WAY OF THE WARRIOR KID III
WHERE THERE'S A WILL...

GI   **NO-GI**

Both types of jiu-jitsu uniforms are awesome in their own ways!

The cool thing when you spar "no-gi" is that you use different skills because you and your opponent DON'T have gis that you can grab.

IMPROVING

It can be very difficult to tell if you're getting better at jiu-jitsu. Why? Because you'll be in a class with kids that are most likely at your same skill level, which means when you learn something new, they just learned it, too. When you learn an armlock, they learn one. When you learn an Americana, they learn one. When you learn a double takedown, they learn one. You're all learning at the same rate. This means when you roll or spar, you're going up against kids that can defend against you because you're all at the same level.

You might expect to suddenly win all the time as proof that you're getting better. Maybe you will, but if you don't, it might not be because you're not getting better, you just need to change up your competition!

You will know just how much better you are when you train against someone who's new or hasn't been training as long as you have. When you train with them, you'll see how the techniques and skills you've learned have made you better and help you outmaneuver and maybe even make them tap out.

WIN OR LEARN

There are tons of reasons why I always say jiu-jitsu is the most AWESOME thing ever! But one of the most awesome things is that it really shows you how valuable the

Warrior Kid "win or learn" attitude is!

And even though you compete alone against your opponent in jiu-jitsu, it is still a team sport, because all the students in an academy help each other get better. Think about it: every time you train with your teammates, you learn from them and they learn from you!

That knowledge is HUGE!

Sometimes you will train against people you are better than, and you can work your moves and help them. Sometimes you will go against kids that are about the same as you, and you can battle it out and learn.

But sometimes, you will train with kids that are MUCH BETTER than you, which is a great way to learn. But when you do go against someone better than you, be ready to be humble! Ha! But more important: be ready to get better at jiu-jitsu.

REPETITIVE

There will be times when jiu-jitsu might seem repetitive. But just like everything we do to stay on The Path—studying, exercising, eating right, saving money, controlling our emotions—repetition helps make us better at those things. But still, whether it's training at jiu-jitsu, studying at school, or cleaning up your room, repetition can seem boring. I've been there! It stinks, but I've also learned how deal with those situations.

MAKE IT FUN

Just like I mention in the earlier section on discipline, sometimes you have to make the situation fun if it seems like it's not! Mix things up! Change things up! Try these tricks on your own!

- Both you and your opponent can spar with your eyes closed.
- One of you can be wearing a gi while the other wears a t-shirt.
- Start out with either you or your opponent in a dominant position and take turns switching so that each of you get a turn in both the dominant and defensive position and see if you can escape!
- Make a rule where you both can only use one arm... or no arms at all!

Ahoy! We be Warrior Kid Pirates and we've come to make you walk the jiu-jitsu plank! A-hardy-har-har!

Guys, costumes aren't the ONLY way to make things fun!

STAY HEALTHY

It's super important that us Warrior Kids stay healthy while we push ourselves at exercising, sports, and martial arts.

Proper supervision when you're doing these things is key. In any sport, good technique and proper form is SUPER important! If you do things incorrectly, you can get hurt and exercise and sports are NOT supposed to injure you. This means making sure a parent, a teacher, or an instructor helps you do them correctly and safely.

Uncle Jake taught me that the human body is actually designed to get stronger and better the more we push it through exercise and sports. Your muscles work like crazy to do what you ask them to do. They actually break down a bit right after you push them through exercise or sports. Pretty intense, right? Well, the good news is that if you're eating right, stretching properly and getting the right rest, your muscles can repair themselves to be STRONGER, which is why it's really important to eat right and not over-train in order to stay healthy!

OVER-TRAINING

If you start to feel really tired or you're not doing as well as you normally do, that is probably your body telling you that you are over-training and you need a rest.

If that happens, instead of doing your usual exercise/sports routine, take a day where you just do a light workout that moves your body around a little bit, works up a sweat, but doesn't PUSH you like your usual routine. If you still feel run down the next day after your light workout, you should probably take a day off—a full rest day. Make sure you fuel your body with healthy foods that make it stronger so it can rebound from over-training.

You can also get mentally tired of training. This is when you feel bored or tired or just plain sick of training, and this also might mean you need a break. Of course, you don't want to just totally fall off The Path if you take a break. Here's a great way to take a break and stay on The Path:

Make an agreement with yourself and your parents that every month you're allowed four breaks—IF you need them. Then sit down and create four tickets with some paper—nothing too fancy—that say "Taking a Break Ticket" on them. Now, if you ever feel burnt out and need a break, go to your parents and hand them one of those tickets—and request a day off. But remember, you only get four per month!

Stay on The Path!

INJURIES AND GETTING SICK

There isn't a warrior alive that doesn't get hurt or sick at some point! It happens. I've had fevers or colds or cut my hands, twisted my ankle, skinned my knuckles, skinned my elbows, skinned my knees, even skinned my nose.

Who skins their nose from training? THIS KID! Ha!

If you get injured or sick, you need to do the right thing. That might mean resting up so you can heal. It might even mean seeing a doctor who tells you to do rehab if the injury is bad enough. No matter how mild or bad the injury, you need to do what you need to do to heal up.

So, if you're forced to rest because of an injury—or maybe you're sick with a cold or flu—you are going to have a bunch of free time on your hands. You might get REALLY bored or restless.

Here's what NOT to do if that happens: do NOT USE it as an EXCUSE to turn your days off into lazy days! DO USE it as an OPPORTUNITY to get smarter or better at another skill! If you are sick or injured, try some of these ideas:

- READ!
- Study about something you are interested in.
- Learn a new skill—something that trains your brain while you can't train your body.
- Create a song, make a drawing, or write a story ABOUT your injury!

SECTION FIVE
LEARN!

Everyone always thinks of warriors as being strong. And that is true—warriors exercise and eat healthy, STRONG foods so they make their bodies as strong as possible.

But guess what? Working to have a strong body is only HALF of being a warrior! The other half is to train our minds so we are as smart as we can be.

I know this is not easy. Just like exercising, sports and jiu-jitsu are sometimes hard. Paying attention in class, studying, doing homework, and reading can seem PAINFUL, SLOW, and BORING!

But guess what? That doesn't matter. Warrior Kids do the right thing no matter how difficult it seems. And guess what else? The ultimate weapon for a warrior is the mind! It is being smart enough to solve problems and overcome challenging situations. You do that with your mind! The smarter you are, the better warrior you will be. That's why the Warrior Kid studies to learn and gain knowledge and asks questions if he doesn't understand.

LEARNING HOW TO LEARN

I'll never forget when Uncle Jake first told me he didn't do very well at school when he was a kid. I couldn't believe it! Uncle Jake not doing well at something? He crushes it at everything he does!!

So what gives?

Well, school didn't seem like something he needed to worry about. He always knew he wanted to be a Navy SEAL, but he didn't think math, science, history, English, art, or other studies mattered when it came to fighting and defeating enemies. But, once he got to be part of a SEAL team, he realized he was wrong! He had to learn a whole bunch of stuff if he ever wanted to succeed. Luckily, he had a boot camp instructor that helped him. The first thing he learned: he had to *LEARN how to LEARN*.

You're probably looking at the page right now and wondering, "LEARN how to LEARN?! What does that even mean, Marc?"

Well, guess what? You're learning how to learn right now, reading this book!

Let me explain...

Learning how to learn means you understand that LEARNING is a PROCESS. That process involves hard work, curiosity, focus, discipline, and patience. It doesn't matter if it's math, jiu-jitsu, mowing lawns, folding laundry, playing basketball, setting the dinner table... no one magically figures out how to do any of those things! You have to learn them! In order to learn them, you have to follow steps. Those steps are called a PROCESS.

Back in fifth grade, I had ZERO idea how to do my times tables. I figured I just stunk at math and was NEVER going to get it. Most of the other kids were doing fine at math. I figured I was just stupid and they weren't.

The only thing that was stupid was me thinking I was stupid!

I just hadn't LEARNED how to LEARN yet. Uncle Jake taught me to use flash cards to learn. I had to make them, I had to organize them, and I had to study them. That was the PROCESS—THE LEARNING PROCESS! I made them by putting a multiplication problem on one side of each card and the answer on the other. When I looked at a card, I guessed the answer. If I was right, I set that card aside. If I was wrong, I put it back in the pile to try again. After about an hour, I had learned to learn my times tables!!

Flash cards helped me go from a fifth grade failure to a math class wiz!

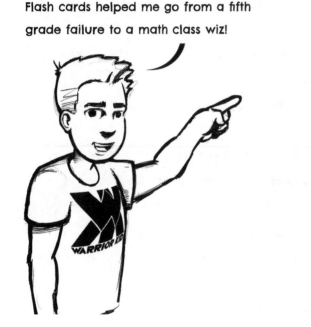

Learning is not easy. You have to read, take lessons, pay attention, and STUDY in class to learn stuff. It's super easy to make excuses and give up on learning. You can decide that you're "not good at it," or that learning is just "too hard." But guess what? That's lazy thinking! Tons of kids think they are not smart—just like I used to think! But that's not true. It just takes HARD WORK!

FLASH CARDS

NEWS FLASH! Flash cards aren't just SUPER-AWESOME TOOLS for learning math. They work for almost EVERYTHING! Here's just a handful of examples of how I've used them:

- Important history dates.
- New words.
- Names of historic people and what they're famous for.
- The capital city for each state in America and every country in the world.
- Jiu-jitsu moves and instructions on how to do them.
- Exercise names and instructions on how to do them.
- Animal breeds and descriptions on where they come from.
- Fun meals and their ingredients and how to make them.
- Chemical elements and their symbols.
- Every country and the world and their flag design.
- National holidays and what they celebrate and what date we honor them.

    I could go on forever, but you get it!!

SOME KIDS...

Most kids (and grown-ups too) are naturally good at a few things—and doing those things comes easily. But there are lots of other things that don't come naturally—and doing them takes lots of work. What comes easy and what doesn't is different for everyone.

Look at me: I've always just naturally been able to draw well. You might not be able to draw, but there might be other stuff you're good at—maybe you have a great talent for memorizing stuff, or you're really good at talking to large groups of people, or you're really good at throwing a football, or maybe you're super funny, or an amazing writer, or you can sing like an angel!

Uncle Jake tells me that sometimes we don't actually find out what we're naturally good at until we're older—so be patient!

He also told me that there is a tiny group of kids that seem naturally good at LOTS of things. Like Danny Rhinehart! He was great at pull-ups, running, school, jiu-jitsu, AND he was SUPER likable. It's easy to get jealous of kids like Danny because so many things seem to come easy to them.

My jealousy of Danny showed me how important it is to control my ego.

FLASHBACK FROM:
WAY OF THE WARRIOR KID III
WHERE THERE'S A WILL...

PERFECT, WAVY HAIR

BIG, WAVING HANDS

NEVER STOPS SMILING

FANCY CLOTHES

FANCY SNEAKERS

Don't get jealous. I made that mistake.

Uncle Jake also told me that kids who are good at lots of stuff sometimes get COMFORTABLE because they are so good at so many things. They think they can coast. That attitude can make them LAZY in the long run. They won't work as hard as you do to learn things. They might not even push themselves to get better at the stuff they're naturally good at! If they don't challenge themselves, they'll never reach their potential.

But you will.

Warrior Kids are willing to challenge themselves and learn things that don't come easy! Don't be afraid of being uncomfortable if it means improving and getting smarter, stronger, healthier, and better!

SCHOOL

How crazy is school?! Think about it for a second... every kid in town shows up to this ONE place and spends the ENTIRE day studying all kinds of stuff. All the classrooms. All the teachers. All the desks. All the books. All the lessons. All the lunches. All the bus rides. All the friendships...

All the LEARNING.

I know school can seem boring at times—and super annoying. But it can also be super fun and exciting. And it's pretty much the most important place for us to learn. Remember, knowledge is POWER. That means school is where Warrior Kids become POWERFUL.

EVERY CLASS. EVERY LESSON.

You probably have classes you like and classes you don't like. It's normal, everyone does. Well, I have some good news! Uncle Jake told me that Warrior Kids don't have to pay attention or try at any of the classes they don't like.

HA! I'm totally kidding!

Uncle Jake actually told me it's SUPER IMPORTANT to try just as hard at the classes and lessons that you don't like as the ones you do like. I know you're thinking, "Why should I try so hard on stuff I have ZERO interest in?" Well, Uncle Jake explained to me that everything you learn makes you smarter—everything.

We're really trying, Uncle Jake.
Even at the classes that aren't fun!

You're on The Path!

Learning fills your brain with facts and knowledge that you can use to solve problems. That is what being smart is: using what you have in your brain to figure things out. Well, the more you put in your brain, the more you can figure out!

You might also be thinking, "Do I really care how many apples Billy had after he ate two of them and gave four away? Why is that kind of math important?"

Well, I'm glad you asked! Because I have an answer!

Uncle Jake told me a story about his good buddy, Dale, who as a kid, really wanted to grow up to be a jet fighter pilot. Dale watched movies about jet fighters, collected pictures of jet fighters, and went with his parents to air shows to watch jet fighter pilots perform super cool tricks. He even got to meet some real-life jet fighter pilots!

Those jet fighter pilots asked Dale how he was doing in math. Dale didn't know what to say—he was terrible at math! He told them he didn't think math mattered when it came to racing around in a jet fighter.

They just shook their heads and smiled. They told him that math has EVERYTHING to do with flying a jet fighter! They explained that pilots need to understand stuff like the number of gallons of fuel the plane has and how far it will get them. They need to be able to calculate how high the plane can fly—how fast it can fly. Plus, pilots may need to land jets on air-craft carriers in the middle of the ocean! If the pilot doesn't calculate speed, distance, and trajectory PERFECTLY...they are going to CRASH!!!!!

They also told him he needed to be really good at science, history, geography, and EVERY other class. And not just good... but *really good* in order to make it as a jet fighter, because only the smartest, strongest, and fastest get picked!

If you want to be a pilot, or ANYTHING in life,
you need to learn a TON of complicated stuff.

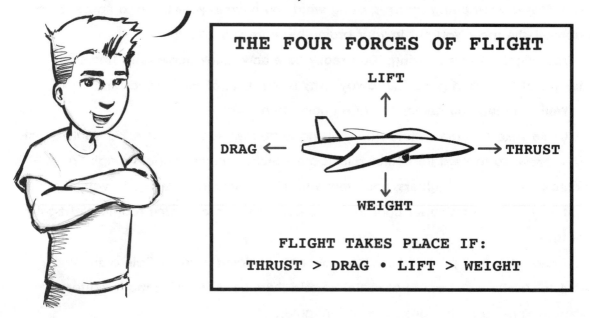

THE FOUR FORCES OF FLIGHT

LIFT

DRAG ← → THRUST

WEIGHT

FLIGHT TAKES PLACE IF:
THRUST > DRAG • LIFT > WEIGHT

After that, Dale pushed himself to get really good at math! He did the same with science, history, geography—ALL HIS CLASSES. Even if it wasn't fun, he knew that learning and doing things that weren't fun would help him get to do the FUN stuff, like fly jet fighters at the speed of sound! He practiced DISCIPLINE and earned the FREEDOM to become jet fighter pilot for Marines Corps! TRUE STORY!!!

PREPARE

Right now, you may not know what you want to be when you grow up. Even I'm not sure! Do I want to be a Navy SEAL like Uncle Jake? Maybe. Do you?

Maybe I'll become a jiu-jitsu instructor and maybe you'll become doctor—who knows?! That means it's even MORE IMPORTANT that we stay disciplined and work hard to learn at every class and every lesson at school so we're prepared for all those possibilities! Remember, Warrior Kids are always prepared—it says so in Warrior Kid Code #6!

SCHOOL TEACHERS

I know teachers might seem a little annoying sometimes! They are always *so* serious! Telling us to pay attention. Making us do all that homework… annoying, right?

Wrong! Teachers are actually pretty awesome. Why? Because they TEACH! Think about it—since Warrior Kids need to always be learning so that our minds are strong just like our bodies—teachers are some of the best people to help us learn!

Every teacher is different—just like every Warrior Kid is different! And just like every Warrior Kid wants to be on The Path to be smarter, stronger, and better, every teacher is on a path to TEACH you how to be smarter, stronger, and better! It's up to us to be the best students we can be.

I know some teachers seem really strict while some are more easygoing. Some teachers make things more fun, while others seem TOTALLY AGAINST any fun! Imagine if all your teachers were easygoing or taught the same way. That would be BORING! It's really good they all teach differently. It keeps us on our toes and on The Path.

IT'S ON US

Uncle Jake told me something very important about teachers. He said that teachers can only do so much to help us kids learn. That goes for school teachers, jiu-jitsu instructors, coaches, parents—even the Uncle Jakes of the world! He said that the responsibility to learn is on us. WE have to study. WE have to work hard. WE have to TRY to learn. If WE don't stay on The Path and do everything we can to get smarter, stronger, and better, then it doesn't matter what our teachers try to teach us.

Remember that.

You definitely DON'T want to be this kid in class.

NOT GETTING CALLED ON

Warrior Kids always ask questions when they don't understand something—especially at school. But sometimes it can seem like your teachers aren't calling on you when you have your hand raised. It happens to me! It's important to not get mad or take it personally. Sometimes the teacher doesn't have time to answer everyone's questions because they have to keep the class schedule moving along. Uncle Jake told me that teachers actually plan out their classes days, weeks—even months—ahead of time! If they stop and answer too many questions during class, they won't get to all the things they planned on before the class ends. That means they have to move the stuff they planned to teach to the next day—which might mean all the important stuff they had planned to teach the next day won't get done. They have to stay on schedule to teach you.

Good news! I have a fix if you don't get your question answered in class! Write down your questions, and after class or during a break, hand them to the teacher. Let them know you need help in getting those questions answered.

They might not give you the answers right away—maybe it'll take a few days—but at least you are asking and showing that you are curious and that you want to learn. Teachers respect students who are hungry to learn!!

HOMEWORK

Pretty much every kid in the world has thought this at least a million times: "Why do I have to do HOMEWORK after I just survived an ENTIRE day of classes and work at school?!"

ANSWER: Because it makes us smarter, stronger, and better!

Remember how doing reps and sets when you're exercising helps your body get stronger? Well, doing homework is like doing reps and sets for your brain. Think about it, you're repeating and practicing what you're learning in each class at school—just like you repeat and practice exercises to get stronger.

If you didn't try very hard to do reps or sets at pull-ups, you'd never get stronger. The same goes for not doing your homework—you won't get smarter if you don't do homework!

ORGANIZE

Warrior Kids are busy kids! Being on The Path means we're pushing ourselves at school, playing sports, and practicing martial arts after school and on the weekends—plus taking care of homework, chores, and making time to hang out with our friends. That's a lot!!

Because we're so busy, it's really important we stay ORGANIZED—and keep track of what we need to do every day.

The best way to do that is to create a daily checklist. A checklist is a list of things you want to do that you cross off as you get them done. Here, let me show you what my to-do lists look like:

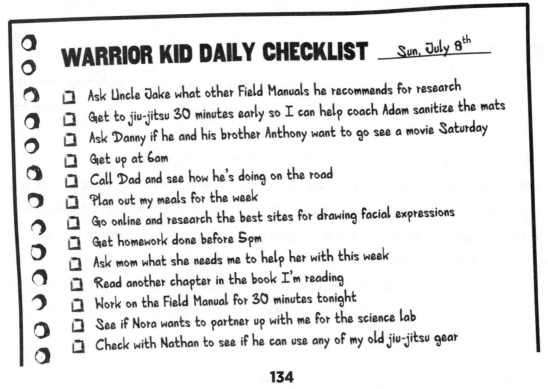

WARRIOR KID DAILY CHECKLIST _Sun, July 8th_

- [ ] Ask Uncle Jake what other Field Manuals he recommends for research
- [ ] Get to jiu-jitsu 30 minutes early so I can help coach Adam sanitize the mats
- [ ] Ask Danny if he and his brother Anthony want to go see a movie Saturday
- [ ] Get up at 6am
- [ ] Call Dad and see how he's doing on the road
- [ ] Plan out my meals for the week
- [ ] Go online and research the best sites for drawing facial expressions
- [ ] Get homework done before 5pm
- [ ] Ask mom what she needs me to help her with this week
- [ ] Read another chapter in the book I'm reading
- [ ] Work on the Field Manual for 30 minutes tonight
- [ ] See if Nora wants to partner up with me for the science lab
- [ ] Check with Nathan to see if he can use any of my old jiu-jitsu gear

Now, creating a checklist is awesome. But it's only half awesome. For FULL awesomeness, you need to keep that checklist somewhere where you are going to SEE IT A LOT during the day. Think about it, if you're busy all day, you might forget about the stuff on your list if it's hidden away from view. So... KEEP IT IN VIEW!

Want to know what I do? I write out my daily checklist on an erasable message board on my bedroom wall AND on a piece of paper just inside the cover on my school notebook.

Remember my suggestion for keeping your Warrior Kid Code handy? Use that same logic–tape your checklist to a book, your refrigerator, or a door in your house... you know what will work best for YOU. Do it!

PRIORITIZE

If you created a checklist right now, would you know what was the most important thing on it? The second most important? The third most important? What about the least important?

Uncle Jake taught me that knowing those things is knowing how to *prioritize*. The most important thing = the highest priority. The least important thing = the lowest priority. It helps sometimes to write out your checklist, take a good look at it and put a number next to each thing to label its priority.

Will "wake up early" be your top priority? Maybe it's "get homework done," or "do fifty pull-ups." Maybe something like "help Dad rake the lawn in the morning" will be the most important because it has to get done super early.

Once you have all your priorities straight, re-write your checklist, now starting it with the #1 priority, then the #2 priority... and work your way down to the lowest priority. Only you can really know how to prioritize YOUR checklist.

You might be looking at your checklist and thinking, "Marc, I know doing my homework is super important. But so is hanging out with my friends! They're both kind of high priorities!" Hey, I get it! Fun times with friends is important—and obviously doing homework is too. Well, Uncle Jake also gave me advice on this exact type of situation. He told me to do the harder, less fun stuff first because delaying the fun stuff will actually help motivate you to get the harder stuff done! It's like a reward—if you focus and get your homework done without any distraction, you get to go hang out and play with your friends! BOOM! Can't beat that Uncle Jake wisdom!

BORED WITH LEARNING

"I'M BORED!!"

How many kids, do you think, have thought that? A million? A billion? A quadrillion?!

I don't know the number—but my guess: EVERY SINGLE KID IN THE HISTORY OF CIVILIZATION!!

But guess what? Boredom is a good thing! I bet you're thinking I'm crazy, but it's true!

When Uncle Jake first told me that boredom is good and that even he gets bored, I thought my ears were broken! Uncle Jake getting bored? He's like an action hero! Well, he told me that EVERYONE gets bored but it's what you DO when you're bored that matters. Some kids, as soon as they get bored doing something, just give up. They look at being bored as a bad thing.

Uncle Jake taught me the importance of looking at boredom as a challenge... an opportunity for us Warrior Kids to challenge ourselves!

Hey, my dudes. Who wants to hang on a couch and stare off into space?

That's going to be a NO, *my dude*.

First you have to ask yourself why you're bored. Maybe you're learning something that seems easy. Maybe you're naturally good in science class and you're reading about the planets and it's all "blah, blah... the Earth revolves around the Sun... blah, blah... the Sun is made up of gas... blah, blah..." And because you're SO GREAT at science, you already got that and it's BORING to go over it. Well, if that's the case, challenge yourself!

How? Dig deeper beyond the "boring" info.

- "The Earth revolves around the Sun." Okay, how about you dig deeper into how many miles it takes to revolve around the Sun? It's 584 million miles!
- So the Sun is made up of gases. Did you ask yourself WHAT gases? It's a mixture of carbon and helium and nitrogen and oxygen and more!

Then dig EVEN DEEPER!

- Ever wonder how much energy the Sun has? Well, the Sun's light creates 430 quintillion watts of energy for the Earth. That's 430,000,000,000,000,000,000 watts! That's INSANE!!
- What's a watt, you ask? Let's dig deeper and FIND OUT!
- A watt is a unit for measuring energy—like you see printed on a lightbulb. A really bright light bulb will require 100 watts to power it.
- That means the Sun's energy could power 4,300,000,000,000,000,000 lightbulbs!

How did I figure that out? You can figure it out, too—just dig deeper with math. Ha!

BORED—BORED

Sure, school and classes can seem boring… but even stuff outside of class—stuff that usually seems like FUN—can get boring. I remember during my sixth grade summer, I had gotten pretty good at school, my lawn mowing business was doing great, and I was crushing it at jiu-jitsu. Things were great! But I just felt… bored with it all.

I told Uncle Jake that it felt weird to be doing great and still feel bored. He told me I was bored because I was *comfortable*. He told me this was good! It meant I had achieved the goals I'd set out for myself. The boredom was my mind telling me it needed a new challenge. I needed to step out of my comfort zone and dig deeper. I need to set greater goals to achieve.

- I had gotten good at jiu-jitsu class and it was getting boring. I could enter into a competition with the goal of finishing in the top three.
- I was comfortable with making $50 a week with my lawn mowing business. I could set a goal of making $100 a week by mowing more lawns.
- I was comfortable with running a sub seven-minute mile. I could set a goal of running a sub six-minute mile.

Want to know something else? THIS BOOK is an example of me digging deeper and setting goals. Uncle Jake's suggestion that I create a Field Manual reminded me how important it is to challenge myself! I was getting comfortable—kind of bored—with where I was on The Path and now I'm writing down what it means to be a Warrior Kid! And here you are reading it! How are you challenging yourself when you get bored?

READING

Uncle Jake told me that reading is one of the most important things a warrior can do to exercise their brain. A smarter brain is a stronger brain. How awesome is that? You can make your brain smarter and stronger just by reading!

I'm sure some of you are thinking, "C'mon, Marc! I already have to read for school, do I really have to read MORE?"

Of course you do!

But guess what? Reading is actually super fun! I'm not just talking about books assigned to you from your teachers in school—I'm talking about reading for YOU. It's like what I wrote earlier about imposed discipline VS self-discipline:

Assigned books from school = imposed reading.

Books you choose to read = self-reading.

Just like any other discipline. READING is FREEDOM!

You can read about ANYTHING you want! What things are you into? Jet fighters? Race cars? Horses? Dogs? Superheroes? Space adventures? Jiu-jitsu? Jiu-jitsu space adventures with superhero dogs?! Hahahaha! I'd read that!

As you start reading about the things you like, you'll notice your brain stores the information you read. Not EVERY BIT, but a good amount. That's your brain LEARNING. Soon, reading will get easier. I remember how surprised I was at all the information I suddenly had in my head from the books I read.

But just like EVERYTHING we do to challenge us as Warrior Kids—don't get too comfortable! Try reading books that challenge you a LITTLE bit, but not too much. And once those books don't seem challenging anymore, read harder books!

Reading is just like EVERYTHING we do to stay on The Path. The more we practice, the better we get at it.

Try some history books that teach you about the past and major events you should know about. Read adventure stories to stimulate your imagination. Read cookbooks to learn what goes into the dinners your parents make. Read biographies of interesting people. Read about geography to learn about the earth. READ EVERYTHING!

READ, NOT RACE

Guess who's been guilty of trying to race through a book as fast as possible? THIS kid! Sometimes, I'm thinking ahead to what I want to do AFTER I read—like exercise or jiu-jitsu. It's easy to do. I'm sure you'll do it too. Try and catch yourself and remember that every page is LOADED with information—and that the writer put that information there for a PURPOSE.

Take your time. Read at a pace that works for YOU. Some kids can read more quickly than others. Some kids need to read very slowly. Everyone is different. You're not smarter just because you can read faster. When you read what you want, take whatever time you need to understand what's on the page.

TAKE NOTES

Do you want to know who takes notes when they read a book so they can understand it better? Uncle Jake! That's right. Even though he's been reading tons of books for years, he still does it! He'll write down notes and circle words or sections that he thinks are super important so that he can remember and understand them better.

- Maybe it's a word he's never seen before and he wants to remember to look it up in the dictionary.
- Maybe it's a section with important, historic dates that he wants to remember and look up online to dig even deeper.
- Maybe it's a section that really inspires him to do something cool, like a new exercise or how to play a new song on his guitar. That's right, Uncle Jake plays guitar!
- Maybe it's something that he wants to remember to share with a friend or get their opinion on.

He's shown me some of his books and a lot of them are ALL MARKED UP! He's written notes on the blank areas, highlighted tons of paragraphs, folded over the corners of every page he wants to read over and over again—it's wild! And guess what? I do it now, too!

Here's a cool way of looking at it. So... in school we all have teachers, right? And lots of times when they're teaching us, we take notes, right? The important stuff that they say is what we need to remember and learn, right?

Write it and you will remember it.

Always take notes!

FLASHBACK FROM:

WAY OF THE WARRIOR KID
FROM WIMPY TO WARRIOR THE NAVY SEAL WAY

Okay—so look at books as little "paper teachers." These paper teachers are teaching you stuff that's just as important as what you are learning in school—so take notes as the book is teaching you!

Here's another cool idea: practice your note-taking with THIS book!

BOOM!!

ALWAYS CURIOUS. ALWAYS LEARNING.

Being on The Path isn't a temporary thing. It's for life. That's right! We're Warrior Kids right now, but that doesn't mean when we get older and are adults that we stop working to get smarter, stronger, healthier, and better. Look at Uncle Jake! He keeps pushing himself to learn ALL THE TIME. He's learning new exercises, new jiu-jitsu moves, new words, new hobbies—all kinds of new stuff! Think about it, when he came to visit me during fifth grade summer, he was actually taking a break from the SEALs so he could go to college in the fall!

He's AWESOME and when I get older, I want to be like him. So, I push myself now to get myself used to it. Because Discipline Equals Freedom, the more I stay disciplined with learning, the more freedom my knowledge will give me, the smarter I'll be when I get older. The smarter I am, the better job and career I'll have... and I'll have a better chance to be able to make an impact in life!

I've learned to not be afraid to ask questions because I KNOW they help me understand things and they help my teachers and parents TEACH ME better.

I've gotten more confident because of all the things I've learned. I KNOW MORE and I can talk about those things with other people and LEARN from THEM!

I could NEVER have written this book if I didn't work really hard to learn stuff. And guess what? This might not be the only book I write! I'm not going to sit back and get comfortable just because I wrote ONE book. Maybe I'll write TWENTY-ONE! I've learned that I need to always be curious and always be learning. We all do. KNOWLEDGE IS POWER!

ATTITUDE

Not only do we Warrior Kids need to exercise our minds to be smarter and increase our knowledge, we also need to train our minds so that we have the right *attitude*. Attitude is how WE CHOOSE to look at situations in life. And our attitude shapes the actions we take in those situations. For a Warrior Kid, having a positive attitude is like having a super power! It protects you and helps you make the right decisions no matter how difficult the situation. But a bad attitude does just the opposite. It actually weakens you and makes things worse—a lot worse!

The Warrior Kid Code helps you create and keep a positive attitude.

Remember, being a Warrior Kid doesn't mean you're supposed to be perfect! If you find yourself having a bad attitude—or your parents or a teacher or a friend tells you that you have a bad attitude—don't freak out! Just turn to your Warrior Kid Code, The Way of the Warrior Kid books, or this Field Manual to help get you back on The Path!

Remember how bad my attitude was in fifth grade? Remember how I viewed my situation and what I thought about everything? I thought I was a loser! I thought I was weak. I thought I was stupid!

But it didn't end there! I also had a bad attitude in sixth grade! I couldn't control my temper with Nathan James. I even blamed HIS bad attitude for creating my bad attitude—meaning I had a double-bad attitude!!

And then during seventh grade I was super jealous of Danny Rhinehart. He actually had an amazing attitude, but not me! I couldn't stand how "perfect" he seemed and my attitude was to try and uncover something about him that would prove he wasn't so perfect. What a bad attitude I had!

I know it's hard to believe but even I can have a bad attitude from time to time.

From *time to time?!*

Remember that for you, me, and every other Warrior Kid out there, our attitudes are going to constantly be tested by new situations, new people, and new problems. So don't get comfortable thinking that having a good attitude in one situation means you're automatically going to have a good attitude in every other situation.

It's a discipline. A good attitude comes from discipline, just like a strong body and a smart mind does. A positive attitude is a Warrior Kid attitude...

SUPER POWER

Just like superheroes have super powers that help them beat the bad guys, a great attitude helps warriors overcome difficult situations! The right attitude helps you accomplish ANYTHING you set out to do.

- You can learn a whole new skill.
- You can overcome your fears.
- You can take charge of any moment and lead.
- You can control your emotions and make sound decisions.
- You can help someone overcome their own challenges.
- You can set an example so that other kids get on The Path.
- You can do ANYTHING!

FACING FEAR

Remember how I was afraid of going in the water during fifth grade? I was pretty much the ONLY kid in school that couldn't swim! It felt horrible!! That attitude only made the situation worse! *EVERYONE* has fears. I do, you do, our parents do, even Uncle Jake does—EVERYONE! It's our attitude about our fears that makes all the difference!

A positive attitude allows Warrior Kids to look at fears as a challenge... a challenge that can be overcome with hard work, repetition, courage, and, of course, discipline!

Uncle Jake helped me understand how to get over my fear of the water by making me face my fear one small step at a time. Each step was designed to help me learn that my fear was all in my head—not in the water! He helped change my perspective and my attitude!

First, he took me to the river, where we would just stand quietly near—but not too close—to the water. At first, I'd be nervous and scared, but after thirty minutes or so, I started to realize that nothing bad or scary was happening. We did this a few more times. Soon I began to notice how tranquil and awesome the water looked instead of sinister and dangerous!

Then for a few visits, Uncle Jake would get in the river while I stood on the edge watching him splash around and enjoy himself. Sure, the first time it made me feel knots in my stomach, but when nothing bad happened, I started to notice that my attitude about the water being THE SCARIEST THING EVER was changing...

Soon, I actually stepped into the river! I didn't go in far, but I did go in up to my knees, with Uncle Jake right by my side. I have to admit I was scared—but not scared like I used to be! Each time we came back I'd go in just a little bit deeper, always with Uncle Jake by my side. Each time I felt myself starting to conquer my fear of the water.

It was all because of the small steps! Each step showed me that there was nothing to actually fear. I kept getting more and more confident and more and more comfortable. Then one day—one HUGE, AWESOME day—Uncle Jake and I jumped in and swam across the river!! It was one of the best days ever!

Later on, Uncle Jake told me that what we did to get me over my fear of the water was called "exposure therapy." That means each step of the process "exposed" me to a little bit more of my fear until I was ready to face it all at once. Pretty awesome, right?!

And guess what? It works for all kinds of fears! I've listed out some below to give you an idea on how it can work! Remember that each step should be done a few days or even a week or two apart to give you time to get over that fear, little by little.

FEAR	STEPS FOR OVERCOMING THE FEAR
Speaking in Front of Your Class	• Read out loud in your bedroom just to yourself. • Read out loud in your bedroom but have one of your parents outside your room with the door closed, listening. • Read out loud in your bedroom with both your parents outside your room with the door closed, listening. • Read out loud in your bedroom with your parents outside your door with the door cracked open just a little bit. • Read out loud in your bedroom with both your parents outside your room with the door halfway open. • Read out loud in your bedroom with both your parents outside your room with the door fully open. • Read out loud in your bedroom with both your parents in your room behind you. • Read out loud in your bedroom, facing both your parents. • Read out loud in your bedroom with your parents and another person who will not tease you—a sibling or a neighbor or a friend. • Read out loud in your bedroom with your parents and even more people.

FEAR	STEPS FOR OVERCOMING THE FEAR
Dogs	• Look at pictures of dogs with your parents on the internet. • Print out pictures of a few different dogs and put them on a table in your room. • A couple days later, hang one of those dog pictures up on your wall. • A couple days later, hang another dog picture on your wall. • A few days later, hang the rest of those dog pictures on your wall. • Visit a dog park with your parents. Stand outside the dog park so you can watch the dogs. • Visit the dog park a few times and watch how the dogs play and have fun. • Have your parents take you to visit one of their friends who has a dog. Have that friend bring their dog out and walk by the car with you inside. • Visit that same friend of your parents but roll the car window down a bit while they walk the dog by your window. • Visit that same friend with your parents but stand outside the car while they walk the dog by you from a distance. • Visit that same friend with your parents and have them walk the dog by you, outside the car, but closer. • Visit that same friend with your parents and have them walk the dog by you but stop and let the dog sit near you. • Visit that same friend and when the dog sits near you, let it smell your hand, and when you feel comfortable, gently pet it.

FEAR	STEPS FOR OVERCOMING THE FEAR
Sleeping With the Lights Off	• Start off going to sleep in your room at night with all the lights on. • Then try going to sleep in your room with just one light on. • Then try going to sleep with all the lights in your room off, but keep your bedroom door wide open and the hallway lights on. • Then try going to sleep with all the lights off in your room and the lights on in hallway, but with your bedroom door left open a little bit. • Next, try sleeping with all the lights off in your bedroom and the lights on in hallway, but your bedroom door completely shut. • Next try going to sleep with your bedroom lights off, the hallway lights off but your bedroom door open.

EGO

Our egos play a huge part in shaping our attitudes. Just like Uncle Jake explained to me in seventh grade, the "ego" is how we see ourselves in the world. It's how we compare ourselves to others... how we view ourselves—good or bad, weak or strong, winners or losers. And it affects how we behave and how we act. Pretty deep stuff, right?

I've learned tons about my ego since I've gotten on The Path. And you know what? My ego has been all over the place! I've had a small ego at times—where I thought I was a LOSER. And I've had a big ego at times where I thought I was the most import-

-ant person ever born in the history of ever! Ha! It's actually really important to have a *balanced* ego, where you aren't too meek, shy, and doubtful about yourself, but also not arrogant, conceded, or overconfident.

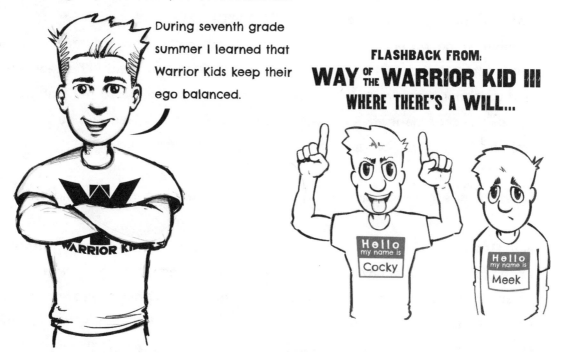

During seventh grade summer I learned that Warrior Kids keep their ego balanced.

FLASHBACK FROM:
WAY OF THE WARRIOR KID III
WHERE THERE'S A WILL...

Let's look at some examples of when my ego was in the wrong place:

- Fifth Grade: My ego and self-confidence were too low! I thought I was dumb, a failure, and a wimp. My ego was small and it I let it shape my attitude. I let Kenny Williamson bully me and I was convinced that I was always going to STINK at EVERYTHING! So... I never had the confidence to try and fix my problems.

- Sixth Grade: I lost my temper all the time with Nathan James. How dare he insult me!?!? I thought I was a super-important Warrior Kid! I blamed HIM for ME losing my temper because I thought I was too good to make a mistake. But really, my ego was too big to let me admit I WAS THE PROBLEM.
- Seventh Grade: My ego was so out of control with jealousy toward Danny Rhinehart! I hated that he was better than me at EVERYTHING, so I lied and I cheated to try and be better than him. My ego was way too big and it affected my attitude—I couldn't accept the truth: it doesn't matter if someone is better, all I can do is control how hard I try to be good at the things I want to be good at.

Let's look at some examples where I actually kept my ego in check and balanced:

- Fifth Grade: After an entire summer on The Path, learning how to be a Warrior Kid, I finally stood up to Kenny Williamson. He could tell when I did that, I was smarter, stronger, and WAY more confident than before! I didn't act all crazy and mad at him. I had the right attitude. I was calm, kept my ego in balance, and he knew that I was not going to run away in fear once I stood up to him. That's why he backed down. And once he did, I was confident enough to be nice to him—instead of turning into a bully myself!
- Sixth Grade: Once I checked my ego and took a look at WHY Nathan teased me I was able to see how difficult his life was. I didn't think I was better than he was—but I did see that I was more fortunate. I decided I could afford to help him try to improve his life. I volunteered both of us to help clean the jiu-jitsu gym and I

helped pay for his membership so he could practice jiu-jitsu and get on The Path.

- Seventh Grade: Once I understood that it's impossible to be the best at everything, and that Danny was actually a super-awesome person who could teach me tons of super-awesome stuff, I got my ego under control. Remember, when Coach Adam named me the captain of our jiu-jitsu team, I asked him to name Danny as my co-captain because I knew his leadership was going to make me a better leader and our team stronger!

As co-captains, Danny and I pushed each other to be stronger and better leaders.

FLASHBACK FROM:
WAY OF THE WARRIOR KID III
WHERE THERE'S A WILL...

CONFIDENCE

True confidence plays a really big role in creating good attitudes. Fake confidence does just the opposite. Acting cocky, arrogant, or talking down to people are examples of fake confidence. Some kids do this to make up for the fact that they actually lack confidence and have small egos. They think that if they portray big egos, no one will know the truth! But it's a mask! So, they act super cocky and treat people terribly. I hate to say it, but Kenny Williamson was like this back in fifth grade.

True confidence creates a balanced ego. A confident kid is calm and kind when faced with a challenge because they BELIEVE they can handle any challenge. A truly confident kid BELIEVES IN THEMSELVES because they put in the practice, the hard work, and the discipline to prepare for that challenge. Think about it. Whether it's a test you've studied for, a game you've practiced for, a jiu-jitsu match you've trained for, or a bully you've readied yourself for: if you're confident, you'll have a positive attitude when you face that challenge!

How awesome is that?!

MORAL COURAGE

Usually when we think of courage and bravery, we think of heroes like firemen, policemen, and soldiers who stand up to danger. The dangers they stand up to are physical ones when they put their bodies in harm's way! It's pretty intense! That is physical courage and bravery.

But there's another type of courage and bravery that Uncle Jake told me about.

It's called *moral courage*. Moral courage is when a person stands up—not to physical danger, but for what's right. Remember in section three of this book when I talked about "the right thing?" Moral courage is about standing up for that.

You might get made fun of. People might even get mad at you, but if you have the moral courage to stand up for what you truly believe is RIGHT, what your parents taught you is RIGHT, and what The Path tells you is RIGHT, then you're standing up for the RIGHT thing! With the right attitude, a Warrior Kid can handle the toughest situations!

TOUGH SITUATIONS

Being a kid isn't easy. We have a lot going on! We're trying to make our parents happy and proud. We're trying to get good grades at school and not get yelled at by our teachers. If we have sisters or brothers, we have to deal with their craziness! Then there's after-school studies and sports. The homework. The chores. The "brush your teeth." The "sit down and be quiet." The "stand up straight." The "it's time to go to bed."

It's a lot!

So when we face tough situations in addition to ALL THAT STUFF, it can be really tough to keep a good attitude! I'm talking about having to deal with people saying mean things. Having to deal with friends that get mad at you over the littlest thing. It could be an accident—like a friend accidentally breaking a window while playing baseball in your backyard, a classmate injuring themselves on the soccer field, or a car accident you see happen on your street.

And sometimes YOU might be responsible for creating the tough situation. Maybe one of your teachers has pulled you aside for misbehaving in class. Maybe you did something that made your sister or brother cry. Maybe you broke ANOTHER glass loading it into the dishwasher!

Any type of tough situation can come out of nowhere and can happen at any time. Us Warrior Kids need to have the right attitude when they happen. We need to be prepared for them. Remember Warrior Kid Code #6 says that we are always prepared and ready for action.

Okay, I'm going to do my best "Uncle Jake" impression and explain what I've learned are the best steps to take in any tough situation!

1. DETACH: Stay calm. You don't want to lose control of your emotions. FREAKING OUT is not an option, even if other people are. Take a deep breath and detach your emotions.
2. EVALUATE: What's the situation? What is your role in the situation? Take stock of what's actually happening and gather information. This is no time to judge or pin blame on anyone. If you're staying calm you should be able to see things clearly.
3. IDENTIFY: What is the right thing to do? Once you've studied the situation, you can figure out what is the best action to take.
4. TAKE ACTION: That's right, once you have figured out what to do, you need to actually take action! Some people freeze instead of taking action. Don't let that happen. Take action. Every situation is different so the action you take will be different.
5. LEARN: After the situation is over look back at what happened. What did you do right? What could you have done better? What did you learn about tough situations in the future?

Okay, so I created (and Uncle Jake helped me!) some examples of "tough situations" on the next page and filled in imaginary details for each of the steps I wrote above.

When situations are at their worst,
you need to be at your best.

DETACH

EVALUATE

IDENTIFY

ACT

LEARN

SITUATION	A SCHOOL BULLY IS PICKING ON A BUNCH OF STUDENTS AND WON'T STOP
Detach	No matter how mean the bully is being, don't take it personally and get mad at them. Anger is the LAST thing the situation needs.
Evaluate	Is the bully a physical danger to the other kids? Has something just happened that caused the bully to act out? How well do you know them and how do they react to being challenged? How can you diffuse the situation and not make it worse? Does a teacher need to get involved or can you handle it?
Identify	So let's say you figured out that you can handle it and that the bully is someone whom you know will back down if they are challenged. As a Warrior Kid you feel confident in your ability to take charge here.
Take Action	You speak up and CALMLY, FIRMLY, and NICELY tell the bully that they shouldn't pick on the students. The bully may tell you to "Get Lost!" The bully might say, "Yeah, and what are you going to do about it?" You have to be prepared to respond accordingly and reasonably with them. Be firm but remember fighting is a LAST RESORT. Get a teacher if you have to.
Learn	Be VERY honest. Did you behave like a Warrior Kid? Did you control your ego? Did you treat everyone with respect? Even the bully? Did you control your emotions and act like a leader? Did your actions help protect the kids getting picked on? Did you help the bully learn to not act like this in the future?

SITUATION	YOUR FRIEND SUDDENLY GETS MAD AT YOU
Detach	Keep control of your emotions. Getting mad is only going to make things worse. Plus you need to be clear-headed to evaluate what is REALLY going on.
Evaluate	Did you do something that may have made them mad? Do they typically overact with emotions and anger as a habit? Did anything happen to them today that would make them sensitive? Are they hungry? Sad? Stressed?
Identify	Let's say you've figured out that it WAS something you said. You were joking about them being lazy. But another kid earlier in the day told them the same thing and they're super sensitive about it. You're going to need to apologize.
Take Action	You need to sincerely apologize. Even if you didn't mean to, you've hurt their feelings. Even if they are mad and not being nice at the moment—you need to apologize. You might be able to apologize right away or you might need to wait until they calm down. Take responsibility for your mistake without blaming them or the situation for YOUR actions.
Learn	Was your apology sincere? Did you keep your ego under control? Did you stay calm when your friend was not? Did you stay humble and accept your friend's frustration? Did you help strengthen the friendship or weaken it with your response and actions?

SITUATION	YOU BROKE A PLATE WHILE DOING THE DISHES
Detach	Don't get caught up in the fact that you might get in a lot of trouble. That will only make you nervous and focus on the wrong things.
Evaluate	Plates are expensive. Is it completely shattered? Do you need to clean up the broken pieces so no one steps on them, or do you need to get your mom right away so that she can decide what to do with the broken plate?
Identify	Let's say that the plate was a gift and is SUPER important to your mom. You don't want to move anything until she sees what happened. This is going to be rough because not only is she going to be upset with you, she's also going to be very sad about the losing the plate. Understand that you will need to control your emotions and take FULL responsibility.
Take Action	Put some things around the area with the broken plate to stop someone from stepping on it. Find your mom. Explain what happened clearly and honestly. Do not makes excuses—accept responsibility. Apologize. Give her time to react. Answer any questions she has. Bring her to the broken plate. If she is mad or sad, let her be mad or sad. Again—NO EXCUSES. You can offer to buy a replacement if one exists. If it's irreplaceable, offer to help her out with extra things around the house to make up for breaking something that was important to her.
Learn	Did you behave like a true Warrior Kid? What could you have done differently to prevent breaking things in the future? Do you understand why your actions were wrong even if it was an accident? Did you truly take full responsibility? Did you make the situation better or worse?

SITUATION	YOU SEE A KID ON YOUR STREET HAVE A BICYCLE ACCIDENT
Detach	Don't freak out. Staying calm and detached is SUPER IMPORTANT as you need to be alert and ready to recall important details, especially if someone is injured.
Evaluate	Okay, ask yourself, what just happened? Replay what you saw over in your mind to help you remember the details. Can you get to the site of the accident safely? Is someone injured? Is property damaged? Who are the people involved? Are there other people at the scene of the accident to help and take charge? Does an ambulance or police need to be called?
Identify	Let's say the kid accidentally bumped into a car that just parked in front of your house. He's fallen down and is crying. You don't know how hurt he is. The driver of the car is an adult you know from your neighborhood. He is outside his car making sure the kid is okay.
Take Action	Quickly get to the scene and introduce yourself and ask both of them if they are okay. Tell both of them that you saw what happened and offer your help. Analyze the situation as best you can in case you need to explain what happened to an adult, the police, or a paramedic. Is the driver sincere about helping the kid? How does the kid seem? If your parents are home, run inside and get them. If not and someone is injured you can call the kid's parents or 911 to send help. If you do, be calm on the phone. ALWAYS control your emotions.
Learn	Did you keep your emotions under control? How well did you do under the stress of the situation? Were you helpful or did you get in the way?

MISTAKES

Everyone makes mistakes and Warrior Kids are no different. The truth is, no one can really control when they are going to make a mistake—because it's a mistake! They happen by accident! So instead of blaming someone for a mistake, instead see what you can do to help so that it doesn't happen again.

If someone else makes a mistake, it is a good time to remember Warrior Kid Code #5. We need to treat people with respect, not judge them, and try to help them whenever possible. Notice that the rule doesn't say "Blame someone!" It says HELP THEM!

Raise your hand if you make mistakes!

There are a couple things I've learned that are SUPER important when it comes to having the right attitude when it comes to mistakes:

1. If someone we know makes a mistake that affects us, we need to forgive them for it.
2. If we make a mistake, we need to apologize to anyone affected by our mistake and learn from it so it doesn't happen again.

FORGIVENESS

We all know how Kenny Williamson and Nathan James purposely did their best to ruin my day. EVERY day. It stopped when I finally got on The Path and stood up to Kenny and finally realized that Nathan was harmless.

Before that... I judged them. I did not like them—AT ALL! But that's because I was letting my emotions and ego take over. I was filled with self-doubt and anger. I thought they were bad and I wanted bad things to happen to them. Once I had the confidence of a Warrior Kid, I could see they weren't bad kids. They were just making bad decisions.

Here's the thing: how many times have I made bad decisions? How many times have I been rude to my mom or dad or another kid in school? The answer: TONS OF TIMES! How many times have you done things that were rude or mean or inconsiderate? It could be throwing a tantrum because you don't want to go to bed or because you didn't want to share the backseat of the car with your brother. It could be making fun of a new kid in class because you want to seem cool and funny! There isn't ONE kid on earth who hasn't misbehaved at some point.

But Warrior Kids are supposed to do the "right thing." Well, if Warrior Kids can misbehave at some point, is it REALLY fair for us Warrior Kids to judge other kids for doing the same thing? To get mad at them? To want bad stuff to happen to them?

I don't think it is. We ALL make mistakes.

NO FREE PASSES

Just because we all make mistakes doesn't mean we should let other kids act terribly or do bad things. And it DEFINITELY doesn't mean we get a free pass to misbehave ourselves because "every kid misbehaves at some point." Ha! No way!

The best thing to do if someone is acting badly is to ask them why they're doing what they're doing. Don't act mad. Don't be aggressive. This isn't about starting a fight. This is about taking a leadership role. Maybe they have a reason—like they're in a rush and so they needed to cut the lunch line. Maybe they just found out their dad is sick and they're scared. Maybe they don't know why they're doing what they're doing.

You can nicely and firmly explain why their behavior or actions are causing a problem. They may understand. They may even apologize.

Having the right attitude when talking with someone who needs to hear that they are doing the wrong thing is HUGE! You don't want to shame them. You don't want to act better than them. Think of it as a conversation to inspire someone who is making bad decisions to get on The Path and make better decisions. Warrior Kids are supposed to help people, and in these cases, you lead by setting a good example and trying your best to NEVER talk down to people.

PARENTS, RELATIVES, FRIENDS, SIBLINGS, TEACHERS

Even the people we love the most can be mean or rude or do things that are definitely NOT GOOD. Even the people we look up to the most. Even the people that we call friends!

- Maybe your mom or dad was in a bad mood because they worked extra-long hours at their job and yelled at you by mistake.
- Maybe your sister or brother punched you in the arm because you didn't give them the TV remote fast enough.
- Maybe your best friend didn't invite you over to play basketball when they DID invite a bunch of other kids to come over and play.
- Maybe your teacher seemed to ignore you having your hand raised so you could ask them to explain a problem you didn't understand.

I could go on forever with examples! No one is perfect. Not even Uncle Jake! So if someone upsets you, just remember no one is perfect. Now, if they've hurt your feelings really badly or you're confused by how they acted, it's okay to ask them why they acted that way. Remember, no free passes! Hopefully they'll explain and they'll apologize. But here's something important: Uncle Jake told me that you can't MAKE someone apologize. You can give someone the opportunity to, and you can ask them to, but they might not. But just like your apologies have to be sincere, so do theirs. Maybe they don't realize they were wrong. Maybe their ego won't let them apologize. So don't force them—it will just make them mad.

APOLOGIZING

It's not easy to apologize, especially if you let your ego get in the way. Sometimes you have to apologize to someone that is SUPER mad at you. Sometimes you have to apologize to someone who did something to you that THEY should apologize for. Like you and a friend had an argument and both called each other nasty names. Sometimes the person you need to apologize to is DEMANDING THAT YOU APOLOGIZE to them!! That's why it's so important to keep your ego and emotions in check. This isn't about YOU. This is about the fact that you have hurt or upset someone. And guess what: situations that call for an apology are usually messy and people get emotional! Warrior Kids control their emotions!

Warrior Kids also help others whenever possible—AND APOLOGIES HELP!

- Be sincere. Talk about what you think YOU DID that was wrong. Don't make excuses. Don't blame them back! Take full responsibility for what YOU did.
- Listen. They may want to talk about what happened. Just because you apologized doesn't mean everything is fixed and you can rush off and do some pull-ups!
- Communicate. Let them know that you understand. Control your emotions and keep your ego in check. Maybe you're expecting an apology from them! But if they don't apologize, it's not an excuse for you to get upset! This is about YOU doing the right thing.
- ACCEPT. They may not be ready to forgive you. They may still be mad at you. I've had people I've hurt or upset stay hurt or upset for a couple days or longer. You have to be patient and let them decide when they choose to forgive you. It's okay!

I've done a lot of things that have gotten people upset at me and they all eventually forgave me.

ARGUING

Arguing is the worst! It usually means that you or the other person is mad. Both of your egos are involved and neither of you want to give in to the other person. Arguing prevents anyone from actually listening to each other. Each person is trying to shout over the other, thinking they're right and the other person is wrong.

You don't want to be like these guys are right now.

173

My friends who have brothers and sisters say this happens all the time between them and their siblings! I've said it a million times: Warrior Kids control their tempers and keep their egos in check! And they LISTEN. Why? Because you learn when you listen. Warrior Kid Code #3 says that The Warrior Kid "asks questions if he doesn't understand."

Think about it. When you argue with someone, it's usually because you both don't understand HOW THE OTHER PERSON CAN POSSIBLY HAVE SUCH A STUPID OPINION!!! Ha! But thinking that way is wrong. Isn't it better to ask why they have the opinion they have rather than judge them? Isn't it better to know why they're mad at you?

Y'know, Nathan. I think it would be helpful if you explained why you're mad at me right now.

I'll give you a hint: IT'S BECAUSE YOU'RE SITTING ON ME!

Maybe you're doing something super annoying that you had NO IDEA you were doing! It's actually a perfect opportunity to LEARN! The more you learn about why people get mad, the better you'll be at understanding future conversations which will allow you to avoid arguments.

It's our egos that get us in trouble! We WANT TO BE RIGHT so badly sometimes—especially if someone is accusing us of doing something wrong. We want to WIN THE ARGUMENT. But if we just control our tempers and look at things as an opportunity to learn—to understand another person's thinking—then we will learn. And if we stay calm in a conversation, we help the other person stay calm. We'll actually get smarter by avoiding arguments—and that is winning. But it is a better kind of winning—winning that makes us smarter and better!

SADNESS

Sadness is a part of life. Just like happiness. Just like anger. Just like fear and just like excitement. And just like every other emotion, it's important to not let it control you. But that doesn't mean we should bury our sadness. While we should control our emotions, it doesn't mean having emotions is wrong—emotions are great. It's how you work through them that is important.

Recognizing red flares is important to controlling your temper, right? If you feel angry or mad it's great to burn it off doing some exercises or going for a run.

If you're having a giggle attack at the dinner table and it's annoying your family, sometimes it's good to walk away and get yourself under control.

If you're scared of something, there's exposure therapy to work your way through the fear.

But what should you do if you're overwhelmed with sadness? Sadness is real. And it hurts. No matter how tough us Warrior Kids are, if a situation is sad, we feel it. Hey, I get really bummed out when Uncle Jake leaves at the end of the summer!

So what should you do if one of your friends moves out of state? What if your family dog or someone you know passes away?

Hey, Marc. You look upset. Is everything okay?

Yeah, something has me feeling sad. Maybe I could talk to you about it... ?

IT'S OKAY TO CRY

It doesn't matter if you're a kid or an adult, a girl or a boy, or if you are a Warrior Kid. People cry when they get sad. That's okay and it is normal. Uncle Jake said he and all his SEAL friends cried whenever one of their friends and teammates died. I asked him what he did to make him feel better, and he told me a few things he did to get through the sadness and not let sadness take over.

TALK

One of the best things you can do if you are feeling sad is talk to other people about it. Friends, family, teachers, coaches, or anyone else that you know and trust. When you talk about what is making you sad, it lets those feelings out. And when you talk about things, you begin to understand them better. So don't be afraid to talk through the subject that is making you sad with the right people.

WRITE

Another thing you can do is write down your thoughts and emotions about what is making you sad. Don't hold back.

Uncle Jake has had super-close friends—best friends—get killed at war. That kind of sadness is HUGE. He knew he couldn't just make it go away. He found that writing a letter to the friend who died helped him work through his emotions.

Now, maybe you're just dealing with someone moving away or your parents are getting divorced, or your favorite gi—the one you won all those tournaments with—got thrown out. It could be anything. We all have different reasons for getting sad and they are all real.

In the letter, Uncle Jake told his friends how much he missed them and how much he was going to miss all the awesome stuff they did. He wrote about all the fun times they had. He also wrote about the hard times. He wrote down everything that he wished he could still tell them. He wrote about how much they helped him be a better person. He wrote that he would always remember them and honor them. While he wrote it, he let himself feel all the emotions that came up. If he felt like laughing, he laughed. If he felt like crying, he cried.

Writing the letter helped him understand WHY his friends were so awesome and why losing them hurt so much. Writing also helped him understand how he could honor their memory going forward. It helped him understand that life is so important and precious.

When he was finished, he would read it to them. Then he would put the letter in an envelope and put it someplace safe. Sometimes he'd go back and read it if he needed to.

TIME HEALS

Over time, Uncle Jake found that while he still missed his friends very much, his memories of them no longer made him so sad. Those memories started making him smile. Those memories fueled him to do everything he could do be smarter, stronger, healthier, and better... IN THEIR HONOR. Uncle Jake knew he was still alive himself and was not going to take that for granted—EVER!

FEELING SORRY FOR YOURSELF

Being a kid is not easy. Sometimes it feels like life is unfair. We get yelled at, picked on, overlooked, bossed around, forgotten, laughed at, and things even worse. It can really create a bad attitude!

My attitude in fifth grade is a perfect example. I pretty much was in a permanent state of feeling sorry for myself.

YOU DO NOT WANT TO BE IN THAT STATE.

Feeling sorry for yourself is the opposite of being a Warrior Kid. It's the opposite of being on The Path. Feeling sorry for yourself is lazy thinking. Don't forget that.

Don't forget how feeling sorry for myself kept me weak. It kept me scared of the water. It kept me thinking I was too DUMB to learn. It kept me eating junk food. Feeling sorry for myself made me a magnet for Kenny's bullying. Feeling sorry for myself STUNK!

Do you want to be that kind of kid? Of course you don't! You're reading this book! You're on The Path! You know that discipline, hard work, patience, repetition, focus, courage, knowledge, smarts, and confidence can help you overcome anything. And if it doesn't, you will LEARN from the experience. If you try your best, you will never EVER have to feel sorry for yourself. Remember that.

DISABILITY. DISEASE. DIFFERENCES

I know I'm lucky to be healthy and have a pretty "normal" life. And I know that for a lot of kids that's not the case. Some kids are born with conditions that affect their health, their minds, or their bodies. Some kids come down with chronic conditions or diseases as they get older. Some kids get injured and find that their bodies or minds don't work as well as they used to.

You might even be one of these kids. If you are, you need to understand that no condition and no disability can stop you from being a Warrior Kid. NONE.

Warrior Kids are kids who wants to do THEIR BEST in life. Whatever you can do—you do it to the best of your ability. You use everything you have to be the best you that you can be.

You know, now that I think about it, there is ONE condition that will stop someone from being a Warrior Kid. Do you know what that condition is?

It is called QUITTING! But, as long as you keep trying to be your best, as long as you don't give up on trying to be better, then you are still on The Path to being a Warrior Kid!

Your journey is YOUR journey. My journey is mine. Uncle Jake's journey is different from mine. Everyone has their own journey. Your journey is about YOU. It's about doing the best YOU can. That is being a Warrior Kid.

Remember that.

EVERYONE'S PATH IS DIFFERENT

RISK

Us Warrior Kids like to challenge ourselves. But we are NOT superheroes. Superheroes are not real! While we are Warrior Kids, we're still KIDS. We need to be careful. We need to have the right attitude when it comes to risk taking and pushing ourselves outside our comfort zone.

Our parents, our teachers, and our coaches have a TON more experience in life. They've learned how to be SAFE and how to do things safely. Like when I jumped off that bridge into the river during the summer! I had Uncle Jake with me to MAKE SURE everything was safe. He was by my side every time I was out at the river working on my fear of water. It would have been dangerous without him there!

I actually needed him by my side the whole time I was learning pull-ups and push-ups! He made sure I did each exercise correctly so I didn't injure myself. I was a rookie! I needed supervision! And so do you!

Don't act like a superhero or a kid that thinks they're *super* tough! Be safe and make sure you have an adult around to supervise when you're pushing yourself physically. Do it!

AWESOME EXERCISES

I thought it would be cool to share some exercises that every Warrior Kid can learn about and try. Notice I didn't say "every Warrior Kid should be awesome at!" Remember, being a Warrior Kid isn't a competition against other kids. It's a competition against yourself as you try to be your best—just like how Uncle Jake said he wasn't trying to be better than other Navy SEALs. He was just trying to be the best Navy SEAL he could be.

Warrior Kids try their best and as long as you are trying, you're on The Path!

Every exercise helps you get smarter, stronger, healthier, and better in a different way—which is why you should learn about them and try them! Pull-ups are going to work totally different muscles than supermans.

You can look up each exercise to find out more about them and REMEMBER to learn proper form, proper technique, and have a parent or another adult supervise you when you participate in any exercise or sport.

Now prepare to bust 'em!

PULL-UPS

1. Step directly underneath the pull-up bar.
2. Look up, reach up, and grab the bar with both hands, palms facing away from you.
3. Grip tightly and lift yourself up toward the bar while bending your knees so that your feet rise up behind you.
4. Raise yourself up until your entire head is higher than the bar. Exhale as you raise up.
5. Lower yourself down slowly, inhaling to fuel your body with oxygen.
6. Repeat lifting yourself up and lowering yourself down until you can't lift yourself up more than six inches. Repeat for 4-5 sets.
7. If you can't do any pull-ups at all, that's okay. Use some of the techniques I explain on page 100 to help you.

PUSH-UPS

1. Get down on all fours with your hands just beyond shoulder width and your feet together.
2. Make sure just your palms and the balls of your feet are contacting the ground.
3. Lower your body slowly to the ground by bending your arms, keeping your back STRAIGHT as a board. Inhale as you do. Do not let your belly sag. Do not let your butt point up in the air.
4. Once your chest and body are just above the floor, push with your arms so that you raise your body back up and your arms are almost straight. Exhale as you do this.
5. Do not lock your elbows. Stop just short of locking them. Pause in this position.
6. Lower your body back down and then raise it back up for as many repetitions as you can. Repeat for 4-5 sets.
7. If you can't do any push-ups with your feet on the ground, then try them from your knees.

SQUATS

1. Stand on flat ground with your feet a little bit wider than your hips.
2. Put your arms straight out in front of you.
3. Keeping your feet firmly planted on the ground, bend at your knees and lower your body. Stick your butt out behind you, your arms in front of you, with your chest pushed out for balance.
4. Lower yourself all the way down. Breath in while you do this.
5. Slowly raise yourself back up to a standing position as you swing your arms back down to your side, to keep your balance. Exhale as you do.
6. Repeat until you cannot do any more with proper form. Repeat for 4-5 sets.

LUNGES

1. Stand straight on flat ground with your feet together and your hands on your hips.
2. Take a big step forward with your right leg and bend at the knee until your left knee almost touches the ground.
3. Stand back up and bring your right leg back even with your left leg.
4. Do the same thing again, but this time, switch so you are taking a big step with your left leg and your right knee almost touches the ground.
5. Repeat, making sure you do the same amount of repetitions for both legs.

STAR-JUMPS

1. Stand straight on flat ground with your feet together and your hands down at your sides.
2. Bend your knees to where you can jump as high as possible into the air.
3. JUMP! As high as you can!
4. When you jump in the air, quickly spread your arms and legs out like a starfish.
5. As you come back down from your jump, bring your feet back together and your arms back down.
6. When you land, bend your knees to absorb the impact, then launch yourself again with another jump.
7. Repeat for as many reps as you can. Do 4-5 sets.

MOUNTAIN CLIMBERS

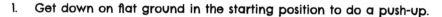

1. Get down on flat ground in the starting position to do a push-up.
2. Keeping your palms firmly on the ground, pull your RIGHT knee up toward your chest so that the ball of your RIGHT foot lands just behind and to the left of your right hand.
3. Next, kick that right leg and foot back to its starting position behind you, while pulling your LEFT knee toward your chest so that your LEFT foot lands just behind and to the right of your LEFT hand.
4. Keep repeating this as if your legs are running but your hands are holding you firmly in place.
5. Repeat for as many reps as you can. Do 4-5 sets.

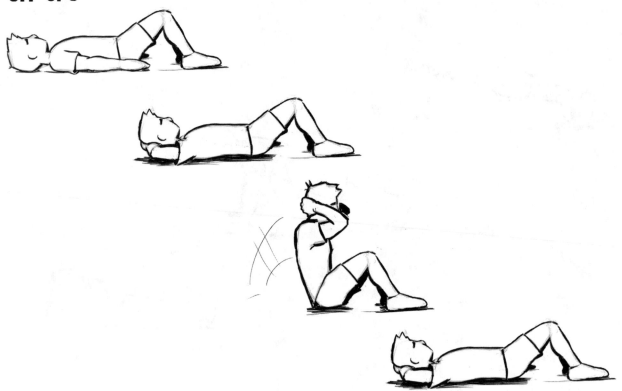

1. Start by lying down on your back on flat ground with your knees bent, your feet flat on the ground, and your hands behind your head.
2. Without moving your feet, legs, or butt, slowly raise your upper body until your elbows hit your knees. Breath out while you do this.
3. Slowly lower your upper body back down to the starting position while inhaling to fuel your body with oxygen.
4. Repeat until you cannot raise your upper body any more. Repeat for 4-5 sets.

SUPERMANS

1. Lay face down on flat ground with your arms stretched straight out as if you're flying like Superman.
2. Raise your chest, arms, and legs off the ground.
3. Hold your feet and hands about 3-5 inches off the ground for 5 seconds.
4. Make sure only your belly and hips are contacting the ground.
5. Breath out while you do this.
6. Slowly bring your chest, arms, and legs back down to the ground, inhaling as you do to fuel your body with oxygen.
7. Repeat for as many times as you can. Do 4-5 sets.

FLUTTER KICKS

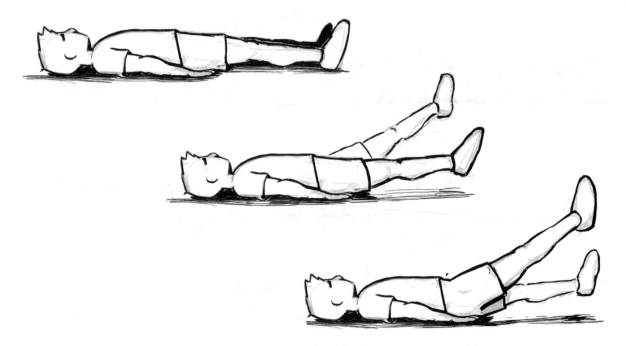

1. Lie down on your back on flat ground with your legs extended and hands tucked under your lower back.
2. Lift your legs and your head off the ground.
3. Swing your right leg up into the air while keeping your left leg still, but off the ground.
4. Now lower your right leg down so it's just up off the ground while swinging your left up into the air.
5. Continue to alternate between legs so that they are fluttering—right leg up, left leg up, right leg up, left leg up...
6. Keep your head raised off the ground as you do. Breath in and out.
7. Repeat until you cannot do any more for one set. Do 4-5 sets.

BURPEES

1. From a standing position crouch down by bending your legs until you can place your palms down on the ground just wider than your shoulders.
2. Keeping your hands on the ground and your arms extended, kick your feet back behind you so that your body is in the starting position for a push-up.
3. Now do a push-up.
4. Then quickly pull your knees and feet back toward your arms, into the crouched position.
5. Then stand quickly and jump straight in the air while swinging your hands above your head.
6. As you return to the ground, swing your arms back to your sides.
7. Lower your body back into the crouch position, legs bent and palms on the ground.
8. Repeat in a quick but smooth manner until you cannot do any more. Repeat for 4-5 sets.

WARRIOR KID DECK OF CARDS WORKOUT

♠ = Burpees
♥ = Push-ups
♣ = Mountain Climbers
♦ = Sit-ups

KENNY   MARC   NORA   DANNY

1. You can play this by yourself or with some friends.
2. If playing by yourself–just try and get through the whole pack in one try!
3. If playing with friends, get a sheet of paper and pen for keeping track and score.
4. Grab a pack of playing cards and shuffle them. Put them face down, at the ready.
5. For each suit in the deck, pick a different exercise to assign to that suit. Example: spades = burpees. Clubs = mountain climbers. Hearts = push-ups. Diamonds = lunges.
6. Write that information down. Also write down the name of each player across the page with plenty of space below to keep track of their scores for every turn they take.
7. The game starts with player one flipping over the top card from the deck.
8. The card's face value and suite determines the exercise and number or reps the player must do to complete their turn.

8. If the card shows a number of 2 through 10, the player does exactly the number or reps shown. If it's a face card or an Ace, here's how many reps to do: Jack = 11 reps. Queen = 12 reps. King = 13 reps. Ace = 20 reps!

9. Example: If a player turns over an 8 of diamonds they must do 8 lunges. If a player turns over a jack of spades they must do 11 burpees.

10. The player is then rewarded points for the number of reps they completed. If a player cannot complete the number of reps the card shows, they are only given points for the reps they've completed—MINUS 5 points.

11. The card is then placed face down in a discard pile and the next player takes their turn.

12. Each player goes in turn until all the cards have been used.

13. Tally up everyone's scores from their turn. Whomever has the highest score wins!

AWESOME FOODS

I've made it pretty clear that we Warrior Kids need to fuel our bodies with good, clean, and healthy food. But as we know sometimes good, clean, and healthy doesn't taste as good as sweet, salty, and greasy junk food!

It takes a lot of discipline to keep a healthy diet. Weird right? You'd think that it would take way more discipline to wake up early, stay organized, or exercise every day. But sometimes eating healthy food can be the hardest! It's because denying yourself something you enjoy is actually REALLY HARD.

DUDE! We're starting to think you don't like us!

It's not that I don't like you. It's that I don't NEED you.

Plus junk food tastes so good when you're hungry!

Just remember that junk foods are not real food. They're actually *WEAK* food. I read that junk foods are actually DESIGNED in a LAB by scientists to taste crazy good! They have tons of sugar and tons of CHEMICALS. They're fake food! And fake is weak. You can't build a STRONG body and a STRONG mind with WEAK food!

STRONG foods like meat, vegetables, fruits, nuts, seeds, and whole grains come from nature—not a lab. Some kids I know don't love the taste of some vegetables. Some kids I know don't like the taste of milk! Some kids I know don't like the taste of fish, chicken, pork, or beef. But vegetables, milk, and protein are important to fueling our bodies... just like doing math is important to getting smart. You may not "like" math but you know it's important, so you study hard to get good at it. Think of all the stuff you don't like but you still do so you can stay on The Path.

Cleaning your room? Probably not the top of your "fun list!"

Doing chores around the house? Definitely not #1 on the "awesome scale!"

Going to jiu-jitsu for the VERY FIRST TIME when you'd rather play video games... well, maybe that one isn't so bad. Ha!

I could go on, but the thing is, if we can get out of our comfort zones to clean our room, then we can get out of our comfort zones when it comes to fueling our bodies and eating STRONG FOODS!

THINK ABOUT WHAT YOU EAT

Once I started learning about what foods were strong and what foods were weak, it made me start to think about what I eat. It doesn't make me an expert though! I follow

Uncle Jake's approach to eating, which is lots of good protein and good, clean vegetables. But even Uncle Jake isn't an expert! I've read tons of stuff about what to eat and what not to eat and there are tons of different opinions.

Want to know what they all agree on? Eat fresh, REAL FOOD and THINK about what you EAT. Is the food you eat making you stronger? Does it give you energy? Are you staying fit with the food you're eating?

Talk with your parents or the adults that take care of you about what you eat and what you're reading in this book. Your parents or those adults are probably going to be your best ally in eating right!

WEAK FOODS

How can you tell if a food is weak, or junk food? One way is to look at the ingredient list on the package. Did you know ingredients are listed from highest quantity to lowest? So many weak foods have sugar or corn syrup right up at the top! That's crazy!!

Here's some tips for knowing if a food is weak, junk, or fake:

- If the ingredient list is SUPER LONG.
- If it has added sugar in the ingredients.
- If it has chemicals in the ingredients.
- If it has "coloring" in the ingredients.
- If it has the word "processed" in the ingredients.
- If it has the word "enriched" in the ingredients.
- If it has the word "preserved" in the ingredients.
- If it lasts forever without going bad.
- If the food looks like it was made by a machine.
- If the food is called "fast food."
- If the food has been fried.
- If the food has a lot of "carbohydrates," which are sugars.
- If the food has extra oils and fats added in.

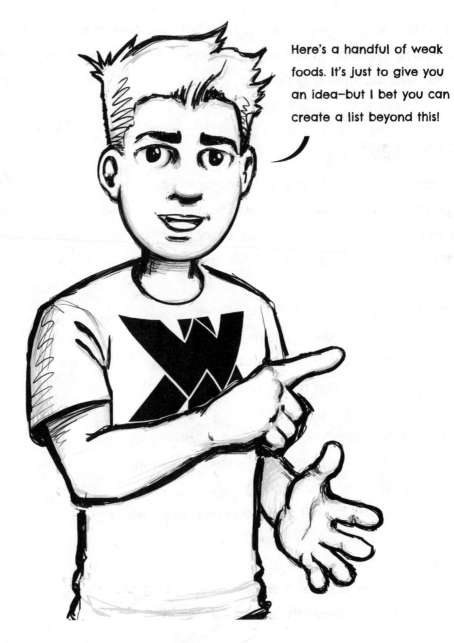

Here's a handful of weak foods. It's just to give you an idea—but I bet you can create a list beyond this!

WEAK FOOD EXAMPLES	
FOOD	**WHY IT'S WEAK**
Cookies.	Sugar, machine made, processed, chemicals.
Chips.	Fried, machine made, processed, added fat, chemicals.
Donuts.	Fried, processed, added fat and sugar.
French Fries.	Fried, high carbohydrates.
Fried Chicken.	Fried, added fat.
Pizza.	Processed, added fat, high carbohydrates.
Cakes and Brownies.	Sugar, processed.
Ice Cream.	Sugar, chemicals.
Milk Shakes.	Sugar, chemicals.
Cheese Puffs.	Fried, coloring, processed, added fat, high carbohydrates.
Soda.	Sugar, chemicals, machine made.
Boxed Fruit Juices.	Sugar, chemicals, machine made.
Pudding.	Sugar, chemicals, machine made.
Pretzels.	Machine made, processed, chemicals, high carbohydrates.
Muffins.	Sugar, processed, high carbohydrates.
Candy.	Sugar, processed.

STRONG FOODS

Want to know how to tell if a food is a *strong* food? Just ask yourself if it comes from nature. Is it grown or raised on a farm? Is the only ingredient the food itself? Strong foods have proteins, healthy fats, and vitamins and minerals in them that fuel your muscles, feed your brain, give you energy, and help you to avoid getting sick. Strong food is REAL FOOD.

Here's some tips on how to recognize strong food:

- It was grown in the earth, on the ground, or in a tree.
- It's a vegetable or a fruit.
- It's a simple, unprocessed meat.
- It has nothing added to it before you buy it.
- Ingredients? You're looking at it!
- It provides the body with protein.
- It provides the body with fiber.
- It provides the body with vitamins and minerals.
- It's fresh—not in a jar, a box, or a bag.

STRONG FOOD EXAMPLES	
FOOD	**WHY IT'S STRONG**
Fish, Chicken, Pork, Beef.	Protein, minerals, healthy fat.
Nuts and Seeds.	Protein, minerals, healthy fat, fiber.
Carrots, Broccoli, Celery and other Vegetables.	Vitamins, minerals, fiber.
Eggs.	Protein, minerals, healthy fat.
Beef Jerky.	Protein, healthy fat.
Peanut and Other Nut Butters (Unsweetened).	Protein, minerals, healthy fat, fiber.
Salads, Leafy Greens and Herbs.	Vitamins, minerals, fiber.
Mushrooms and Sweet Potatoes.	Vitamins, minerals, fiber.
Milk.	Protein, vitamins, minerals.
Mozzarella, Feta, Cottage and Soft Cheeses.	Protein, vitamins, minerals, healthy fat.
Blueberries, Strawberries, and Other Low-Sugar Fruits.	Vitamins, minerals, fiber.
Yogurt.	Protein, minerals.

SOME OTHER FOODS

There are some other foods that have both strong qualities and weak qualities. These are foods that have good, strong stuff in them like lots of vitamins or protein–but they also have some weak stuff in them–like lots of sugar or bad fats.

Listen, I really like bananas–they're high in potassium, which is a mineral that's HUGE for fueling your body. But they do have a TON of sugar and too much sugar is not good for you–even if it's in fruit. So I only eat a few bananas every week–as a treat or reward after I've done something to earn a reward. Moderation is a word Uncle Jake uses. It means DON'T GO CRAZY with something. So, moderation it is! Can you think of any foods like those below that have both strong qualities and weak ones?

OTHER FOOD EXAMPLES		
FOOD	**WHY IT'S STRONG**	**WHY IT'S WEAK**
Bananas.	Vitamins, minerals, fiber.	Sugars.
Oranges.	Vitamins, minerals, fiber.	Sugars.
Rice, Beans, Grains.	Vitamins, minerals, fiber.	Processed, high carbohydrates.
Bread, Pasta.	Vitamins, minerals, fiber.	Processed, high carbohydrates.
Honey, Maple Syrups.	Vitamins, minerals.	Sugars.
Hard Cheeses.	Protein, vitamins, minerals.	Bad fat.

TASTES BAD

Tons of kids tell me that they want to eat healthy but that when they try some stuff—like broccoli or eggs or field greens or fish... every bone in their body just goes, "YUUUUUUUUUCK!!"

I get it! It's totally WEIRD when you start eating food that isn't DESIGNED to taste delicious in a lab! That's because you've gotten used to FAKE food packed with SUGAR and CHEMICALS! You're not ready for the NATURAL taste of REAL FOOD.

Real food tastes... *real*.

Listen, the first time I ate spinach I thought I was going to PUKE!! HA! Seriously. It tasted pretty, well... *GREEN*. Luckily I was already on The Path and I knew that spinach was good for me. So while I wanted to like it, I wasn't *ready* to like it. Yet.

I asked Uncle Jake for advice. And he gave me a great idea THAT WORKED!!

CAMOUFLAGE

If you're trying to eat something that doesn't taste good to you, just camouflage—or disguise—its flavor with a food that DOES taste good to you. Let's say you're trying to eat broccoli. Take the broccoli and mix cheese or butter or bacon—something you LIKE the taste of—into it. All you want to do is make the broccoli taste better. Do this every time you have broccoli for a month or two. Now, here's the important part: every time you camouflage the broccoli with the other food, use a little LESS of the good tasting food. Over time, you'll be masking the flavor of the broccoli less and less. By the end of the two months you'll actually be eating broccoli on ITS OWN. BOOM! Bring on the next healthy food you don't like the taste of! Here's how I got over some healthy foods that I didn't love the taste of at first:

- Salmon. I used to put mustard on it!
- Spinach. I used to put ketchup and cheese on it!
- Yogurt. I used to put honey or blueberry jam on it!

A LACK OF GOOD FOOD CHOICES

There are going to be times when there are just not any good, healthy, and strong foods to eat. Maybe it's because your parents have been too busy to buy fresh groceries and you're eating something out of a box or from takeout. Maybe you're at a friend's house and they just don't eat healthy, strong food like you do. Maybe you're at a birthday party and it's all cake, candy, and chips.

It's not a big deal when this kind of stuff happens. Just go with it. You don't want to complain and you don't want act like you're SOOOOOO IMPORTANT that you MUST HAVE GOOD FOOD TO SURVIVE!! Ha!

First off, Warrior Kids don't complain. They find solutions. They also don't blame others—they *help out others when they can.*

So be appreciative that SOMEONE IS FEEDING YOU. And if you're at a celebration, it's fine to eat some cake and join in on the fun! It's about the birthday boy or girl, NOT YOU and your Warrior Kid diet. It wouldn't be fair for you to make a fuss.

Treat those moments as the FREEDOM that comes from DISCIPLINE, enjoy them, and then get back on The Path!

SECTION NINE
YOU ARE THE LEADER

Congratulations! You've made it to the last chapter in my Warrior Kid Field Manual! What do you think? Has it made sense so far? Is it helpful? Like I've mentioned, I started writing this because Warrior Kids want to help people and I want to share the lessons I've learned from all the crazy stuff I've been through—all the stuff I've learned from Uncle Jake and my experiences on The Path.

And that's what this book is really about. Passing it on. Maybe my book will help you think about your own journey on The Path and you will decide to be a leader to other kids. Why not?!! Seriously, if you're on The Path and all this stuff makes sense to you and you practice it... then you're totally ready to lead!

How awesome is that?!

CHARACTER

When it comes to being a Warrior Kid and when it comes to being a leader, it doesn't matter whether you're a boy or a girl, tall or short, rich or poor. Your nationality doesn't matter. Your race doesn't matter. What you look like doesn't matter. What DOES matter is how YOU ACT AS A PERSON. How you carry yourself. How disciplined you are. How fair you are. How hard you work. How much you push to LEARN. It's about how dedicated you are to doing the right thing and how willing you are to do ANYTHING you ask anyone else to do.

All that stuff makes up your character. It's the most important part of being a leader. Doing the right things for the right reasons. If you do that, your character will be strong, and people will follow you.

WOLVES

Uncle Jake once told me a cool story about wolves and wolf packs. He told me about the way wolves go about leading. He said that in lots of ways, animals and people behave similarly. Wolves live in packs and people kind of live in packs too.

The wolf that leads the pack is called the alpha wolf and they're usually the biggest, strongest, and smartest wolves in the pack. But alpha wolves don't get to lead just because they're the biggest and the strongest and the smartest. The reason they lead is because they know HOW TO LEAD. They protect the pack. They help the pack find food. They know when to defend the pack against danger and when to walk away from danger. Now, if the alpha wolf is mean or a bully, if it is selfish or lazy, then the other wolves will gang up on it and replace it with a better alpha wolf that knows HOW TO LEAD. Uncle Jake told me that the PACK plays just as much of a role in leading as the alpha. Each wolf gets its strength from the pack. They travel together and protect each other as a team. But at the same time, the strength of the pack comes from each individual wolf playing their role on the team and working together. It's about balance. It's about working together.

I'M STANDING NEXT TO A WOLF!!! How cool is this?!
Wait a second. This is actually EXTREMELY dangerous...

For a person to be respected as a leader, they have to be like a GOOD alpha wolf. They need to take good care of their team and work WITH that team. They should be a good person. They should encourage each member of the team to do what they do best. They should listen to the team. They should FOLLOW the team... not just LEAD them!

IT'S TIME

Do you feel ready? Nervous? Excited? Scared?

Good. Ha!

Because it is time. And you should feel ready, nervous, excited, and scared about leading. That stuff is going to keep you ENGAGED and pushing against failure. And DISCIPLINE is going to keep you prepared. It's going to give you the freedom and confidence to lead.

Are you thinking, "Whoa, whoa, whoa, Marc! I still have a bunch of questions about this leadership stuff!"

Good! Ha!

If they're not answered by my Field Manual and if they're not answered by the Way of the Warrior Kid books, then you're going to need to find those answers *for yourself* on The Path. As you go through your OWN JOURNEY as a Warrior Kid, you'll get the answers to your questions. Maybe they'll come from your parents or your teachers. Maybe they'll come from your instructors and coaches. Or maybe those answers will come from talking to other Warrior Kids!

Or maybe the answers will come from YOU.

As you lead. As you follow.

As you win. As you learn.

And by the way, you started leading the moment you got on The Path and started following the Warrior Kid Code! It may not seem like it because it all happens step by step. But the moment you made that decision to do what it takes to be a Warrior Kid... you started leading *yourself.*

How far are you on The Path right now? How far am I? Who knows?! What I do know is that we're both on it. And we're on it for a reason. For the *right* reasons.

And if we both started leading the moment we got on it, then imagine what we can do the longer we stay on it.

So, stay on The Path.

YOU ARE THE LEADER.

- Marc

Make Sure to Check Out

WARRIORKID.COM

and

JOCKOSTORE.COM

For all your Warrior Kid updates, news, and gear!

and

Click the "Ask Uncle Jake" button at warriorkid.com/podcast
to submit your question for Uncle Jake to answer on the podcast!

Follow The Warrior Kid on Instagram and Facebook
@WAYOFTHEWARRIORKID